MASTERING STOICISM

FROM BEGINNER TO ADVANCED PRACTICES IN STOIC
PHILOSOPHY FOR RESILIENCE, INNER PEACE, AND
WISDOM

ADRIAN COLE

CONTENTS

THE BEGINNER'S GUIDE TO STOICISM

THE PHILOSOPHY OF STOICISM

THE BEGINNER'S GUIDE TO STOICISM

EMBRACE ANCIENT WISDOM TO OVERCOME MODERN STRESS AND ANXIETY

INTRODUCTION

Have you ever felt overwhelmed by the chaos of modern life, unsure of how to find peace amidst the noise? If so, you are not alone. Stress, anxiety, and a pervasive sense of dissatisfaction frequently punctuate our daily existence. However, what if I told you that an ancient philosophy could offer you the tools to cope and thrive in today's world?

Stoicism is a school of philosophy that dates back to ancient Greece and Rome. It focuses on building resilience, finding inner peace, and controlling one's reactions to external events. It teaches us that while we cannot control every aspect of our lives, we can control our sensitivities to them, which in turn can dramatically improve our well-being.

My journey with Stoicism began with skepticism. As someone deep-rooted in the challenges of modern life, I initially doubted how knowledge from thousands of years ago could ease my contemporary woes. However, through trial and error, I discovered not only the practicality of Stoic principles but also their profound effect on my mental health and overall happiness.

This book aims to clarify Stoicism for beginners, as it guides you through the basic concepts of Stoic philosophy and provides you with manageable phases to integrate its wisdom into your everyday life. You don't need a background in philosophy to begin—just an open mind and willingness to explore how these ancient concepts can address modern problems.

You, the reader, are probably an adult seeking a reliable and philosophical approach to personal growth and stress management. Perhaps you've noticed Stoicism's growing popularity in discussions about mental health and well-being and are curious about how to apply it to your own life. This book is for those intrigued by the practical benefits of a philosophical life.

In the following chapters, we will explore the core beliefs of Stoicism, examine the lives of notable Stoic thinkers, and provide practical exercises that you can implement immediately. Each part of the book builds on the previous one, creating a comprehensive roadmap from theory to practice.

This book combines historical insights, practical exercises, personal anecdotes, and practical research to ensure a well-rounded and engaging learning experience. By blending these elements, I aim to make Stoicism not only relatable but also proven in its effectiveness in improving your life.

By the end of this book, you won't just understand Stoicism; you will have started living it, finding in its ancient wisdom a path to a more serene and resilient life. Embrace this journey of transformation, where you will equip yourself with enduring Stoic strategies to navigate the complexities of modern life with clarity and resilience.

1

LAYING THE FOUNDATIONS OF STOICISM

At the heart of every philosophy lies the promise of a better way to live, a plan for navigating the complexities of living with a steadier hand and a more serene mind. Stoicism, perhaps more than any other ancient philosophy, extends this promise not through abstract theorization but through practical, easy-to-understand wisdom. As we explore this philosophical giant, it's vital to understand that Stoicism isn't just about enduring hardship—it's about transforming our reactions to hardships, thus changing our lives for the better.

Some of the most influential figures in history, including George Washington and Thomas Jefferson, drew deeply on Stoic principles to guide their decisions. This timeless appeal underscores the adaptability and enduring relevance of Stoicism, making it as appropriate in the bustling streets of today's metropolises as it was in ancient marketplaces.

WHAT IS STOICISM? UNDERSTANDING ITS ORIGINS AND CORE BELIEFS

Defining Stoicism

Stoicism is a school of classical Greek philosophy that began in Athens with Zeno of Citium around 300 BC and continued throughout the Roman and Greek world until approximately the 3rd century AD. It is more than just a set of beliefs; it is a way of life that emphasizes ethics, the discipline of the will, and the logic of the natural world. The Stoics focused on practicality—an aspect that made this philosophy accessible and practical for both scholars and common people in ancient times.

Built on the foundation of understanding what we can control and what we cannot, the central aim of the Stoic doctrine is to achieve a state of inner peace and resilience, regardless of external circumstances, by mastering one's own emotions and actions. This core principle helps individuals focus their energy and attention on their actions and attitudes, which are in their power to change, rather than external events that are not.

The Core Beliefs of Stoicism

At the core of Stoic philosophy are several fundamental beliefs: the logic of the universe, the discipline of desire, and the acceptance of fate, all of which govern emotional responses. Stoics believe that by understanding the nature of the world and our place within it, we can learn to accept the moment as it presents itself, respond with reason rather than emotion, and, therefore, maintain tranquility.

Stoics endeavor to live in harmony with nature, acknowledge that everything is interconnected, and that human reasoning is part of the divine intellect. This alignment with nature involves not only gratefulness for the natural world but also an understanding of life's ebb and flow, accepting both successes and failures with calmness. Stoicism teaches that distress comes not from events themselves but from our feelings about them, a viewpoint that empowers individuals to cultivate inner strength and flexibility.

Historical Context

The historical and social contexts of the Hellenistic period, marked by warfare, political upheaval, and cultural shifts, significantly influenced the development of Stoicism. This era saw the shattering of Alexander the Great's empire and the rise of the Roman Empire, both times of momentous uncertainty and change. Stoicism offered a sense of calm and stability, proposing that despite external chaos, individuals could achieve inner peace through self-control and rational thinking.

Stoicism's strength and pragmatism were further consolidated as it spread to Rome, where thinkers such as Seneca, Epictetus, and Marcus Aurelius adapted its principles to guide leadership, governance, and personal conduct amidst the complexities of empire.

Connecting to Modern Relevance

The principles of Stoicism have found a new connection to today's fast-paced, high-stress environments. The Stoic focus on controlling one's reactions to peripheral events reflects the challenges faced by modern individuals dealing with the pressures of daily life. In an age where anxiety and external pressures are rife, the Stoic practice of focusing on what is within our personal control—our thoughts, behaviors, and reactions—delivers a powerful tool for managing stress and enhancing satisfaction in our lives.

Through Stoicism, you can learn to detach from the chaos that surrounds you, approach life's challenges with a calm mind, and respond to every situation with thoughtfulness and integrity. In embracing these principles, you engage in a proven strategy that has supported individuals through tumultuous times for centuries, offering not just a philosophy of endurance but a path to thriving no matter what life throws your way.

THE ART OF DIFFERENTIATING BETWEEN CONTROL AND SURRENDER

One of the most transformative aspects of Stoicism involves understanding and applying the Dichotomy of Control, a principle that succinctly divides the elements of our lives into two clear categories: those we can control and those we cannot. This principle, at its core, teaches that our thoughts and actions fall within our sphere of control, while external events and the actions of others do not. By internalizing this distinction, we not only enhance our ability to cope with life's challenges but also set the stage for genuine personal growth and increased satisfaction.

Consider a typical day: you might get stuck in traffic, have a disagreement with a colleague, or face unexpected delays in a planned project. In each scenario, the Stoic practice would involve identifying elements you can control—your responses and actions—and recognizing those you cannot, such as the behavior of other drivers, your colleague's opinions, or the timing of external approvals. This differentiation is crucial because it shifts the focus from frustration over uncontrollable outcomes to proactive management of your reactions and choices. For instance, while you cannot clear the traffic, you can choose to listen to a podcast or an audiobook, transforming a stressful commute into a productive or enjoyable time. In the workplace, rather than stewing over a disagreement, you could decide to articulate your viewpoints clearly and seek common ground, thereby fostering a collaborative rather than confrontational atmosphere.

To practically apply this concept in daily life, consider maintaining a daily journal. Each evening, reflect on the day's events, categorizing them as 'within my control' and 'beyond my control.' This exercise not only aids in reinforcing the Stoic dichotomy but also cultivates a habit of mindful reflection. You might write about the traffic and note your decision to engage in a more rewarding activity, thus focusing on your control over your reaction rather than the external situation. Over time, this practice boosts a shift in perspective, where you naturally begin to engage more with your sphere of influence and less with the uncontrollable.

The psychological benefits of this Stoic practice are profound—engaging consistently with what we can control while surrendering to what we can't leads to a significant reduction in anxiety and stress. This is mainly because much of our societal anxiety stems from a perceived lack of control over external events. When we realign our focus towards areas where we have genuine influence, such as our personal efforts and attitudes, we feel not only more empowered but also more peaceful. This empowerment fosters a proactive attitude toward life; rather than being reactive to situations, we become active participants in shaping our own well-being.

Moreover, integrating the Dichotomy of Control into your life equips you to handle adversity with superior calm and resilience. When faced with professional setbacks or personal trials, a Stoic approach prompts you to assess which aspects of a situation you can influence. If a project at work is criticized, instead of harboring resentment or doubt, you might choose to seek constructive feedback and focus on improving your skills, thus converting potential negative energy into a catalyst for personal and professional development. This mindset, rooted in Stoicism, transforms challenges into prospects for growth, ensuring that you keep your composure and purpose regardless of outside pressures.

Embracing the Dichotomy of Control is fundamentally about nurturing a deep sense of inner stability and self-assurance. It teaches us that while we may not always have control over the events that develop around us, we hold the final authority over how we respond. This is empowering, placing the reins of our emotional and mental well-being firmly in our hands. As you continue to practice this Stoic principle, you will notice a shift not only in your reactions but in your overall approach to life—a shift towards a more deliberate, thoughtful, and resilient life, not grounded in the chaos of the outside world but in the clarity of your rational choices.

EXPLORING THE STOIC VIRTUES: WISDOM, COURAGE, JUSTICE, AND TEMPERANCE

The Stoic philosophy is built on a foundation of virtues that guide the ethical range of its followers—Wisdom, Courage, Justice, and Temperance. Each of these fundamental virtues is not only a trait to be developed in isolation but is interrelated, supporting and enhancing each other in the cultivation of a balanced and principled life.

Defining the Cardinal Virtues

Wisdom in Stoicism is regarded as both practical and philosophical knowledge. It involves the ability to navigate complex situations with clarity and ethical insight, distinguishing between good, bad, and indifferent actions based on their true nature and potential consequences. Courage goes beyond physical bravery to encompass moral and psychological resilience—the strength and integrity to face internal conflicts, ethical dilemmas, and life's unavoidable sufferings. Justice comprises the fair treatment of others, rooted in kindness, social responsibility, and community service, while recognizing the inherent value of all human beings and striving to act in ways that benefit both the individual and the community.

Temperance is the practice of self-control and moderation, guiding one to make choices not determined by passions or desires but aligned with one's best logical interests.

Connecting Virtues to Daily Life

In the daily grind, these virtues translate into actions and decisions that shape the quality of our lives and our interactions with others. Consider a professional setting: applying Wisdom might involve choosing the most effective and ethical approach to a complex project and recognizing the long-term impacts over short-term gains. Courage is called upon when we must speak up about workplace issues or advocate for changes that align with our moral values despite potential opposition or risk. Justice is practiced through fairness in dealings with colleagues, ensuring that everyone's contributions are acknowledged and valued and that decisions are made with consideration for their effects on all stakeholders. Temperance manifests in managing our ambitions and work-life balance, ensuring that our pursuit of professional success does not compromise our health or personal relationships.

At home or in personal settings, these virtues are equally vital. Wisdom guides parents when imparting ethical values to their children. Courage enables individuals to confront personal fears or challenges, perhaps addressing long-standing personal issues or making significant life changes that, while daunting, promise substantial personal growth. Justice plays a role in how one contributes to one's community, perhaps through volunteer work or advocacy, while Temperance can help one manage personal finances and resist the lure of indulgences that might lead to harm.

Highlighting the Interconnection of Virtues

The development of one virtue often aids the enhancement of others. For instance, true Courage is not reckless but is guided by

Wisdom, which assesses risks and determines the worthiness of a cause. Justice is informed by Courage, as it often requires bravery to ensure fairness and equitable treatment in the face of societal pressures. Similarly, Temperance can prevent the pursuit of justice from turning into zealotry, reminding us to seek balanced solutions that benefit the broadest community. This interplay ensures that the practice of one virtue reinforces and elevates the others, promoting a well-rounded approach to personal and moral development.

Encouraging Self-Assessment

Understanding and developing these virtues starts with self-assessment, which involves honest reflection on one's current strengths and areas for growth. You might find yourself naturally aligned with Justice, perhaps easily engaging in community service or advocacy, yet struggle with Temperance, finding it difficult to say no or to moderate desires that lead to excess. By identifying these natural inclinations and areas of challenge, you can focus your efforts on cultivating balance, ensuring that no virtue is left underdeveloped.

Engaging in regular self-reflection can be facilitated by keeping a virtue journal, where daily or weekly entries focus on actions taken, decisions made, and their alignment with Stoic virtues. Such a practice not only enhances self-awareness but also encourages proactive living that consistently aligns with Stoic ideals. Over time, this reflective practice can deepen your understanding of how these virtues operate in your life and how you can consciously integrate them into your daily actions and broader life decisions.

In essence, the Stoic virtues offer a framework for living that promotes not only personal well-being but also the welfare of others, creating a ripple effect that extends from individual actions to collective harmony. By striving to embody wisdom, courage, justice, and temperance in all aspects of life, we engage in a continuous process of ethical refinement and personal growth that is both challenging and deeply rewarding.

EUDAIMONIA: THE STOIC CONCEPTION OF A FLOURISHING LIFE

At the heart of Stoic philosophy lies the pursuit of Eudaimonia, a term that resonates deeply through the ages, embodying the highest human good. But what exactly is Eudaimonia? In its simplest translation, it means 'flourishing' or 'happiness'; however, in the Stoic context, it denotes a quality of life achieved through the cultivation of virtue and rational living. Unlike the fleeting pleasures sought in hedonistic pursuits, which are often dependent on external circumstances and can lead to ephemeral satisfaction, Eudaimonia represents a state of enduring well-being that emanates from a life lived in harmony with one's rational nature.

The distinction between common notions of happiness and Stoic happiness is crucial and profoundly liberating. While contemporary society often equates happiness with external success—wealth, popularity, and luxury—Stoicism invites us to shift our focus inward. It teaches that true happiness is found not in external acquisitions or sensory pleasures but in developing the inner virtues —wisdom, courage, justice, and temperance. This form of happiness is stable and sustainable because life's inevitable challenges and changes do not easily disrupt it.

Achieving Eudaimonia requires more than intellectual understanding; it necessitates practical engagement with life's daily demands through a Stoic lens, which involves consistent reflection on one's actions, ensuring they align with personal and moral values. For instance, consider the practice of journaling, a method embraced by many Stoics, both ancient and modern, as a way to reflect on one's daily experiences and evaluate them against Stoic principles. This habit encourages mindfulness and self-correction, fostering a life that not only espouses virtue but actively practices it.

Moreover, aligning life with one's values in the Stoic sense means prioritizing actions and choices that enhance personal virtue and contribute to the common good. It involves asking oneself regularly, "Is this action just? Does this decision support my growth in temperance? Am I exercising courage in this challenge?" Such questions guide the Stoic practitioner towards actions that are not only personally beneficial but also socially responsible, thus expanding the scope of Eudaimonia to include the well-being of the community and relationships.

Historical and contemporary anecdotes abound with examples of individuals achieving Eudaimonia despite challenging circumstances. Consider the case of Admiral James Stockdale, who was held captive during the Vietnam War. Stockdale credited his survival and resilience to the principles of Stoicism, particularly the works of Epictetus, which he had studied prior to his capture. His ordeal included severe hardship and uncertainty, yet his commitment to Stoic principles provided a framework for maintaining mental clarity, moral integrity, and, ultimately, a profound sense of personal fulfillment, even in captivity. His experience underscores the Stoic belief that external conditions do not define our happiness or our capacity to live a fulfilling life.

In more everyday contexts, consider a professional who practices Stoicism in the midst of a volatile career in a high-stress environment. By focusing on maintaining integrity, using rational judgment, and managing personal reactions to workplace dynamics, this individual cultivates a professional life that not only achieves the external metrics of success but also maintains internal peace and ethical standards, thus embodying the Stoic ideal of Eudaimonia.

Embracing community and relationships is also vital in the pursuit of Eudaimonia. Stoicism teaches that humans are inherently social creatures, and our well-being is deeply connected to that of others. Engaging positively with our communities—whether offering support during difficult times, participating in community-building activities, or fostering environments of mutual respect and understanding—enhances our sense of connection and shared humanity. This engagement not only enriches our own lives but also reaffirms our commitment to the Stoic principles of justice and fairness, fostering a broader social environment where Eudaimonia can flourish.

Thus, the path to Eudaimonia is not a solitary trek but a dynamic interaction with the world, guided by rational principles and a commitment to virtue. It is a state continuously cultivated through thoughtful actions, reflective practices, and meaningful engagements with others. In this way, Stoicism offers not just a philosophical view of happiness but a robust, practical framework for living well. Whether facing adversity or celebrating success, the Stoic pursuit of Eudaimonia provides a steadfast compass, ensuring that every aspect of life is approached with wisdom, integrity, and a deep-seated tranquility that comes from living in alignment with one's deepest values.

2

THE STOIC PHILOSOPHERS: LIVES AND LESSONS

As we delve deeper into the essence of Stoicism, it becomes evident that the lives of its philosophers are as instructive as their teachings. Among these venerable figures, Seneca stands out not only for his philosophical insights but for his tumultuous life, which serves as a profound lesson in resilience and inner peace. His experiences, fraught with political intrigue and personal hardship, paired with his thoughtful writings, offer a rich source of guidance for anyone facing the vicissitudes of modern life.

SENECA'S INSIGHTS ON RESILIENCE AND INNER PEACE

Seneca's Personal Challenges

Lucius Annaeus Seneca, commonly known as Seneca the Younger, navigated a life replete with extremes of wealth and deprivation, power and peril. His career in the complex and often perilous world of Roman politics saw him rising to the height of influence as an advisor to Emperor Nero, only to be cast into exile in Corsica under Claudius. This exile, prompted by accusations of an affair with

Caligula's sister, was a period of profound personal suffering and introspection for Seneca. Yet, it was also during this time that he composed some of his most poignant works on Stoicism, reflecting on the nature of adversity and the human condition. His eventual return to Rome and subsequent rise to power did little to secure his safety, as he later faced forced suicide by the increasingly paranoid Nero. Through all these fluctuations of fortune, Senecas's writings and actions reflected a deep commitment to Stoic principles, emphasizing resilience, ethical integrity, and the pursuit of tranquility amidst turmoil.

Teachings on Resilience

Seneca's writings, rich with personal reflections on his own experiences, offer timeless insights into the cultivation of resilience. In his moral essays and letters, he frequently discusses the importance of resilience in the face of adversity, advocating for a perspective that views obstacles not merely as misfortunes but as opportunities for growth and affirmation of character. For instance, in his *Letters from a Stoic*, Seneca advises, "The bravest sight in the world is to see a great man struggling against adversity." His letters to his friends and political contemporaries are replete with advice on maintaining composure and integrity no matter the external circumstances. He teaches that true resilience stems not from avoiding adversity but from engaging with challenges in ways that refine and affirm one's virtues.

Modern Application of Seneca's Resilience

In today's context, Seneca's thoughts on resilience have profound implications, especially when dealing with professional setbacks or personal losses. Imagine facing a sudden career setback, such as a project failure or job loss. Applying Seneca's principles, you would focus not on the loss itself but on your response to it. This might involve viewing the setback as a chance to reassess your career path, develop new skills, or strengthen your professional network. Similarly, in the face of personal loss, Seneca's advice would guide you to seek consolation in the acceptance of life's impermanence and to find peace by cherishing memories and lessons learned from loved ones.

The Role of Inner Peace

For Seneca, resilience is linked intricately to the achievement of inner peace. He postulates that true peace comes from within and is not disturbed by external chaos. In his view, one can achieve inner peace through the acceptance of fate and the understanding that suffering and hardship are part of the human experience. This acceptance is not passive resignation but an active, rational acknowledgment that enables one to maintain composure and clarity of thought in any situation. For Seneca, the cultivation of inner peace involves a daily practice of reflection, self-examination, and deliberate choice to respond to life's challenges with equanimity and reason.

Visualization Exercise: Finding Your Stoic Center

To integrate Seneca's teachings into your life, try this simple visualization exercise. Find a quiet place and take a few deep breaths to center yourself. Visualize a recent event that caused you distress. Now, reimagine the event from a Stoic perspective, focusing on your control over your response rather than the event itself. Ask yourself what virtues you can apply to this scenario, such as patience, courage, or wisdom. Reflect on how changing your response could change the outcome, both externally and internally. This exercise can help you cultivate a more resilient and peaceful approach to the challenges you face.

Through his life and writings, Seneca provides a compelling example of how Stoic philosophy can be lived out, even in the face of extreme adversity. His insights into resilience and inner peace offer valuable guidance for navigating the intricacies of modern life, teaching us that by focusing on our internal responses and cultivating tranquility, we can face any circumstance with clarity and strength.

MARCUS AURELIUS: A DAY IN THE LIFE OF A STOIC EMPEROR

Imagine the sun rising over the ancient city of Rome, its first light casting long shadows behind the marble columns of the Imperial Palace. It is here that we find Marcus Aurelius, not only the ruler of a vast empire but also a devoted Stoic, weaving the principles of this philosophy into the very fabric of his daily life. His days, rigorously structured yet reflective, serve as a profound example of how Stoicism can infuse one's duties with wisdom, balance, and ethical rigor.

Marcus Aurelius's mornings would likely begin before dawn, a time reserved for solitude and the first of his meditative practices. Here, in the quiet predawn hours, the emperor reflected on the day ahead, mentally preparing himself to meet his responsibilities not just as a ruler but as a Stoic. These moments of reflection were crucial, allowing him to align his actions with his values, ensuring that each decision was made not in pursuit of personal glory but for the greater good of his people. His commitment to Stoicism profoundly influenced his approach to governance, emphasizing justice, temperance, and the welfare of others above the easy temptations of power and luxury.

Duties of state consumed the bulk of his day—meetings with military leaders, discussions with advisors, and the endless adjudication of disputes. Yet, even amidst this whirlwind of activity, Marcus Aurelius remained a philosopher at heart. His Stoic viewpoint was evident in his measured responses and the deliberate pace he engaged with each issue, embodying the Stoic ideal of thoughtful deliberation. He often reminded himself and those around him that the role of a leader is to serve, a concept deeply rooted in Stoic ethics. Each decision, each law passed, and each conflict resolved were seen through the lens of how they served the common welfare, reflecting his unwavering commitment to justice and virtue.

Marcus Aurelius's Meditative Practices

Integral to Marcus Aurelius's daily routine were his meditative practices, which were not only personal reflections but also formed the basis of his writings in *Meditations*. These writings, a series of personal notes, thoughts, and reminders, offer a window into his soul, revealing a man who sought wisdom and virtue in every aspect of his life. *Meditations* is not a philosophical treatise but a personal journal filled with his struggles, insights, and resolutions. In passages where he writes about accepting the things he cannot change or focusing on his improvements rather than criticizing others, we see his commitment to Stoic principles, such as the dichotomy of control and the importance of self-mastery.

These meditations were likely penned during quieter moments, perhaps in the evening, as he reflected on the events that had transpired during the day. They served as a kind of self-dialogue, a way for Marcus Aurelius to counsel himself to stay true to his Stoic path amidst the immense pressures of Imperial life. His writings emphasize the importance of self-reflection, a practice that allowed him to remain grounded and maintain inner peace despite the external chaos of political life.

Leadership Lessons from Marcus Aurelius

The leadership style of Marcus Aurelius, heavily influenced by his Stoic beliefs, offers timeless lessons in ethical and effective governance. His reign, often marked by fairness and a genuine concern for the well-being of his subjects, stands in stark contrast to the frequently tyrannical rule seen in other Roman emperors. His approach underscores the Stoic belief that power should be exercised with responsibility and restraint and that the measure of a true leader is not the extent of their power but how they use it to benefit others.

Modern leaders can draw significant insights from his example, particularly in the realms of business and politics, where ethical challenges are rampant. Marcus Aurelius's emphasis on virtue and integrity in leadership, his focus on serving rather than ruling, and his commitment to personal ethical development are principles that can profoundly influence contemporary leadership practices. In a world where leaders are often swayed by personal ambition or external pressures, the Stoic model advocated by Marcus Aurelius offers a compelling alternative, promoting a leadership style that is both morally grounded and effective.

Examining His Legacy

The legacy of Marcus Aurelius extends far beyond his reign as emperor. His life and writings have influenced countless individuals across the centuries, reinforcing his status not only as a political figure but as a philosopher-king. His embodiment of Stoic principles, particularly under the strain of Imperial responsibilities, offers a powerful example of how philosophy can be lived in practice, not just contemplated in theory.

His impact on Roman society was profound, instilling values of justice, temperance, and rationality at a time when such qualities were often overshadowed by corruption and decadence. Moreover, his writings in *Meditations* have endured as one of the most precise expressions of Stoic philosophy, providing guidance and inspiration to those seeking to understand and implement Stoic principles in their lives. Through his example, Marcus Aurelius remains a beacon of how one can wield great power with great responsibility, guided by the wisdom of Stoic philosophy. His life reminds us that the true test of our principles is not how we wield them in tranquility but how we hold to them in times of adversity.

EPICTETUS ON FREEDOM AND THE ILLUSION OF CONTROL

Epictetus, whose origins starkly contrast with the philosophical stature he eventually attained, offers one of the most compelling narratives in Stoic philosophy. Born into slavery in the Roman Empire, Epictetus's early life was marked by limitations and hardships that anyone might assume would constrain his spirit. However, his journey from being a slave to a revered Stoic teacher underscores a fundamental Stoic belief: true freedom is a state of mind, not a physical condition. This belief shaped his teachings, which profoundly influenced not only his contemporaries but also countless individuals across centuries.

Epictetus's philosophy centers on the dichotomy of control, a concept that he spoke of with profound clarity and simplicity. He taught us that understanding what we can control and what we cannot is the first step toward freedom. In his discourses, he famously stated, "Some things are in our control and others not." The things in our control are our opinions, aspirations, desires, and the things that repel us. These areas are where we have real power. In contrast, things we cannot control include our bodies, possessions, reputation, and social status—elements that are often mistakenly viewed as sources of freedom or power.

This teaching is revolutionary because it shifts the focus from external acquisitions or conditions to internal strength and resilience. For Epictetus, the essence of freedom lies in mastering one's internal state, cultivating virtues, and responding to external events with wisdom and equanimity. This perspective is incredibly empowering, suggesting that regardless of one's external circumstances—whether one is a CEO, a middle manager, or a recent graduate entering the workforce—the capacity for personal freedom and effectiveness lies fundamentally within.

Applying Epictetus's ideas on freedom and control can profoundly impact how individuals navigate both personal and professional challenges today. In the professional realm, consider the scenario of facing an unexpected layoff or substantial organizational changes—situations typically loaded with uncertainty and stress. Rather than being consumed by the anxiety of the unknown or fixating on the instability, you can apply Epictetus's teachings by focusing on your response to the change. This might involve proactively seeking new opportunities, enhancing your skills, or even reassessing your career path to align more closely with your core values and interests. By focusing on these areas—clearly within your control—you not only maintain a sense of personal agency but will also turn potential adversity into a catalyst for growth.

In your personal life, Epictetus's philosophy can be equally transformative. Consider personal relationships, which often involve complexities that can lead to frustration or unhappiness. Epictetus would advise focusing on your individual actions and reactions—elements you can control—rather than attempting to change the other person. This approach fosters healthier relationships built on understanding and respect for personal boundaries rather than conflict and the futile desire to control others.

The implications of Epictetus's teachings for personal empowerment are profound. His life is a testament to the idea that external conditions do not define us; instead, our internal responses to those conditions shape our freedom and happiness. This perspective encourages a proactive approach to life, where challenges are seen not as barriers but as opportunities to reinforce and express our values and virtues. It teaches that personal empowerment stems from mental discipline and philosophical insight—qualities that enable us to navigate life's changes with confidence and poise.

Epictetus's narrative and teachings continue to resonate because they address a universal quest for freedom and happiness—a quest that is as pertinent today as it was in ancient times. His emphasis on internal control, coupled with the practical strategies he proposes, provides a robust framework for living a fulfilled and free life, regardless of external circumstances. By internalizing and applying these principles, you can cultivate a resilient and empowered approach to both personal and professional challenges, embodying the true spirit of Stoic freedom.

MODERN STOICS: HOW TODAY'S THINKERS APPLY ANCIENT WISDOM

The resurgence of Stoicism in contemporary society is not merely a revival but a vibrant reinvention, adapting ancient wisdom to suit the needs and challenges of the modern world. Today, a diverse array of philosophers, writers, and thought leaders have embraced Stoic principles, infusing them into their work and daily lives. These modern Stoics not only interpret Stoic philosophy for today's audience but also actively demonstrate its relevance and applicability across various fields.

One notable figure in the realm of modern Stoicism is Ryan Holiday, whose works such as *The Obstacle Is the Way* and *Daily Stoic* have introduced Stoic philosophy to a broad audience, emphasizing its usefulness in overcoming personal and professional challenges. Holiday's writings distill complex Stoic concepts into actionable advice, making them accessible and applicable to readers worldwide. His approach underscores the Stoic belief that obstacles are not impediments but opportunities for growth, a message that resonates deeply in today's fast-paced, challenge-laden world.

Similarly, Massimo Pigliucci, a philosopher and author of *How to Be a Stoic*, embodies the practical application of Stoicism through his blend of personal anecdotes and philosophical discourse. Pigliucci explores the ethical and practical dimensions of Stoicism and encourages readers to live a more thoughtful and reflective life. His work not only elaborates on the theoretical aspects of Stoicism but also provides concrete examples of how to apply these principles in everyday situations, from handling stress at work to managing personal relationships.

The influence of Stoicism is also evident in the field of psychology, particularly in the development of cognitive-behavioral therapy (CBT), which shares many principles with Stoic thought. The work of Donald Robertson, a cognitive-behavioral therapist and author of *The Philosophy of CBT*, illustrates how to integrate Stoic techniques for managing thoughts and emotions into modern therapeutic practices. Robertson's integration of philosophy and psychology demonstrates the adaptability of Stoic ideas, proving that they can provide robust frameworks for mental health and well-being in the 21st century.

In the business world, Stoicism has been adopted by leaders and entrepreneurs who use its teachings to foster resilience, ethical leadership, and a balanced approach to success. Tim Ferriss, an entrepreneur and author, frequently discusses the impact of Stoicism on his approach to business and personal productivity. By advocating for practices such as the "fear-setting" exercise—which involves defining and confronting fears to overcome procrastination and take calculated risks—Ferriss showcases how to effectively utilize Stoic principles to achieve professional success and personal fulfillment.

The global Stoic community has seen significant growth, facilitated by the rise of digital platforms and social media. Online forums, blogs, and virtual conferences have allowed individuals from various parts of the world to connect, share experiences, and learn from each other, fostering a sense of global connection and shared human experience. These communities provide a space for ongoing dialogue and collaboration, ensuring that Stoic philosophy remains a living, evolving tradition. Through podcasts, interactive webinars, and online courses, modern Stoics continue to explore and expand the boundaries of Stoic philosophy, making it relevant to diverse audiences and contemporary issues.

As Stoicism continues to inspire and influence people around the world, it is clear that this ancient philosophy retains its power and relevance. Its principles of resilience, rationality, and virtue offer timeless solutions to modern problems, providing individuals and communities with the tools they need to lead more thoughtful, productive, and meaningful lives. The work of modern Stoics not only preserves the legacy of ancient thinkers like Marcus Aurelius and Seneca but also enriches it, proving that Stoic wisdom is not confined to the past but is a living, breathing guide to living well in the present.

As we close this exploration of modern Stoicism, it is evident that the echoes of ancient Stoic thought continue to resonate through time, adapted by contemporary voices into a robust framework for living in today's complex world. The lessons drawn from both historical and modern Stoics provide us with invaluable insights into the art of living, emphasizing that true contentment and success are achieved not through external achievements but through the cultivation of virtue, resilience, and rationality.

In the next chapter, we will delve into practical Stoicism, examining specific tools and techniques that you can apply in your everyday life to harness the full potential of Stoic philosophy. Join us as we explore how to turn philosophical insights into everyday actions, bringing Stoicism into the heart of your daily experiences and interactions.

3

PRACTICAL STOICISM: TOOLS FOR TODAY

In the hustle of everyday life, where decisions loom large from the moment you sip your morning coffee to when you switch off the bedside lamp, how do you ensure that your choices are not just reactive but reflective and aligned with your deepest values? This is where Stoicism, far from being a dusty relic of the past, strides into the contemporary arena with clarity and purpose. It offers not just a way of understanding the world but the practical tools for navigating it. As we delve into the practical aspects of Stoicism, you'll discover how to simplify complex decisions, apply effective frameworks, and see the benefits of these practices through real-life applications.

SIMPLIFYING STOIC PRINCIPLES FOR DAILY DECISION-MAKING

Stoicism teaches us that the essence of good decision-making lies in recognizing what is within our control and what is not. This understanding is crucial because it liberates us from the frustration of trying to influence what we cannot change and directs our energy toward what we can actually affect. By distilling Stoic principles into simple, actionable advice, we can make this wisdom a substantial tool in our daily lives.

One effective way to apply Stoic wisdom is by using the Dichotomy of Control to assess situations. When faced with a decision, ask yourself: "Is this within my control?" If yes, you proceed with actions that can influence the outcome; if no, focus on your response to the situation instead. This straightforward framework can dramatically simplify the decision-making process by clearing away unnecessary concerns and concentrating your efforts on areas where you can make a real impact.

Consider a common scenario: a disagreement at a family gathering. Here, you cannot control the opinions or emotions of others, but you can control your responses and actions. A Stoic approach would be to remain calm, listen actively, and respond with respect and clarity, aiming for understanding rather than victory. This not only reduces personal stress but often leads to more productive and harmonious interactions.

Another area where Stoic principles prove invaluable is in career decisions. When contemplating a job change, for example, focus on elements such as preparing your resume, acquiring new skills, or networking—factors you can control. Worry less about the fluctuating job market or the decisions of potential employers, as these are outside your direct influence. This approach not only makes the process less daunting but also enhances your preparedness, making you a more compelling candidate when the opportunity arises.

Regular reflection is the key to reinforcing these decision-making frameworks. Engage in a nightly review where you examine the decisions you made throughout the day, assessing them through the lens of Stoic principles. This practice not only deepens your understanding of Stoicism but also embeds its wisdom into your daily routine, gradually transforming your approach to decision-making.

Reflective Exercise: Evening Review

Each evening, take a few moments to reflect on a significant decision you made that day. Write it down in a journal and evaluate it:

- What aspects of the situation were within your control?
- How did you respond to those aspects?
- What were the outcomes, and how do they align with your Stoic values? This simple exercise can provide profound insights into your decision-making process and help cultivate a more Stoic approach to daily challenges.

By embedding these simplified Stoic principles into your daily decision-making, you not only make life more manageable but also more meaningful. The clarity that comes from focusing on what you can control, paired with the ethical framework provided by Stoic qualities, equips you to handle life's complexities with confidence and composure. This chapter will continue to explore practical Stoic tools that you can incorporate into various aspects of your daily life, enhancing both your personal growth and your impact on the world around you.

THE STOIC MORNING ROUTINE: STARTING YOUR DAY WITH SERENITY

Imagine greeting each day not with a rush of anxiety or a barrage of unchecked emails but with a moment of serene contemplation. A Stoic morning ritual can provide just that—a structured start to your day that centers your thoughts and grounds your actions in Stoic wisdom. Such a routine often involves meditation, journaling, and the reading of Stoic texts, each action woven together to cultivate a mindset of calm and clarity.

Meditation, in the Stoic sense, involves a focus on mindfulness and presence. This practice isn't just about tranquility but about preparing the mind to face the day's challenges with a focus on what you can control. You might spend a few minutes each morning in quiet reflection, considering the day ahead and reminding yourself of your capacity to meet it with composure and rationality. This daily meditation helps anchor you in the present, steering your mind away from "what ifs" and worries about the future that can so often unsettle your day before it even begins.

Journaling, too, plays a crucial role in the Stoic morning routine. This isn't simply about recording events but about reflecting on your interactions and thoughts through the lens of Stoic philosophy. What virtues were you able to practice yesterday? What could you have handled more wisely? What are today's opportunities for practicing Stoicism? These morning entries can help you set a deliberate tone for the day, one that aligns with Stoic ideals such as wisdom, justice, courage, and moderation.

Reading Stoic texts each morning, whether from Marcus Aurelius' *Meditations* or Epictetus' *Enchiridion*, serves as a daily reminder of the principles you aspire to live by. These readings provide philosophical insights that can be thought over throughout the day, serving as a guide in times of difficulty or decision. The words of these Stoic philosophers remind us of the resilience and moral fortitude we can aspire to, providing both comfort and challenge as we start our day.

This structured start is not about rigid adherence to a checklist but about creating a space for mental and emotional preparation. It's about starting the day with a ritual that reinforces your values and centers your mind, setting a tone of calm and purpose. These moments of morning serenity are not just pauses in the rush; they are investments in a more thoughtful, effective, and balanced way of living.

Throughout the day, the practice of visualization can extend the benefits of your morning routine. Before each significant event or decision, take a moment to visualize the upcoming situation. See yourself handling the scenario with composure and adhering to Stoic principles. What would wisdom look like in this meeting? How can courage show itself in this conversation? This practice not only prepares you for the day's challenges but also strengthens your ongoing engagement with Stoic ideals.

Numerous individuals have found that implementing such a morning routine significantly enhances their daily experience. Consider the testimony of a school teacher who discovered that starting the day with Stoic meditation and journaling allowed her to handle classroom challenges with much more composure and empathy. Or a business executive whose morning routine of reading and reflection led to more thoughtful leadership and decision-making. These stories underscore the practical benefits of a Stoic morning—enhanced calm, improved decision-making, and a day constantly aligned with one's deeper values.

Incorporating these practices each morning sets a foundation of tranquility and intention, providing you with the tools to navigate the day's complexities with Stoic calm and wisdom. Whether you face professional challenges, personal decisions, or unexpected difficulties, a morning grounded in Stoic practice prepares you to meet each with equanimity and resolve. This is the power of a Stoic morning: it does not change the external world, but it profoundly transforms your ability to engage with it, fostering a day lived with intention, virtue, and peace.

STOIC RESPONSES TO COMMON WORKPLACE CHALLENGES

The modern workplace can often feel like a battleground where headaches such as looming deadlines, difficult coworkers, and the ever-present fear of job insecurity conspire to disrupt our peace of mind. Stoicism, with its focus on inner tranquility and rational response, offers powerful tools to navigate these common challenges. By understanding and implementing Stoic strategies, you can transform the way you interact with your work environment, maintaining both effectiveness and calm in the face of daily workplace pressures.

One predominant source of stress in any job is the pressure of tight deadlines. The anxiety of racing against the clock can not only diminish the quality of your work but can also lead to burnout. Here, the Stoic practice of focusing on effort rather than outcome can be particularly beneficial. Instead of fixating on the deadline itself—a factor often outside your complete control—concentrate on doing the best work possible in the time available. This shift in focus aligns with the Stoic principle of accepting external events as they occur while maintaining control over your actions and attitudes. By doing so, you not only enhance your peace of mind but often your efficiency as well.

Interpersonal conflicts with coworkers also pose significant challenges in the workplace. Stoicism teaches us that other people's behaviors and opinions are outside our direct control and, thus, should not dictate our inner state. When dealing with difficult colleagues, apply the Stoic strategy of objective judgment—view these interactions as opportunities to practice patience and understanding. Before reacting, pause and consider the intentions behind their actions, which often stem from their personal challenges or insecurities. Responding with empathy and maintaining professional decorum not only diffuses potential conflicts but also fosters a more positive work atmosphere.

Job insecurity is another stressor that can cause significant anxiety, given its direct impact on our livelihood and future plans. Stoicism addresses this fear by reminding us of the transience of all external conditions and urging us to find security within ourselves. Cultivate an 'inner citadel' by developing skills and a mindset that enhances your employability and adaptability. Focus on building a robust professional network and staying updated with industry trends, making you better prepared to handle whatever career changes may come. This proactive approach not only mitigates fear but also empowers you to take charge of your career trajectory.

Assertive Communication in the Stoic Workplace

Effective communication is critical to managing workplace stress and fostering a collaborative environment. Stoicism, which promotes clarity of thought and expression, can significantly enhance your communication skills. When expressing your needs or setting boundaries, do so with clarity and respect, ensuring your message is understood but not imposed. For instance, if a project's deadline is leading to an unreasonable workload, calmly explain the situation to your manager, propose viable solutions, or request additional resources. This method of communication—not aggressive but assertively clear—ensures that your professional boundaries are respected while maintaining positive relationships with your colleagues.

The concept of the 'inner citadel' is particularly relevant when developing resilience against workplace stress. This Stoic metaphor describes a mental fortress that protects your rational and emotional core from external disturbances. Building your inner citadel involves regular self-reflection, practicing mindfulness, and adhering to your ethical values, which together fortify your psychological resilience. With a strong inner citadel, you can face workplace challenges without losing your composure, making decisions that reflect both your professional judgment and your Stoic principles.

By applying these Stoic strategies to everyday workplace challenges, you not only enhance your professional effectiveness but also contribute to a healthier, more harmonious work environment. These practices allow you to navigate the complexities of your job with a calm and focused demeanor, turning daily challenges into opportunities for personal and professional growth.

BUILDING EMOTIONAL RESILIENCE THROUGH STOIC REFLECTION

Emotional resilience, from a Stoic perspective, is defined as the capacity to endure life's challenges with a steady demeanor, adapt to changing circumstances, and recover effectively from adversity. This resilience is not a passive acceptance but an active engagement with life's difficulties, approached with a rational and balanced mindset. Stoics believe that our reactions to adversity (not the events themselves) shape our experience and character. By managing our responses with wisdom and equanimity, we cultivate a resilience that not only helps us endure but also thrive.

Reflective practices are integral to developing Stoic resilience. These practices, such as evening self-examinations or reviews of daily actions and reactions, serve as tools for introspection and self-improvement. They allow you to dissect your day, understand your emotional responses, and assess how well your actions align with Stoic principles like courage and justice. For instance, consider a day when you faced significant professional criticism. Through Stoic reflection, you would examine not just the feedback itself but your response to it. Did you meet it with defensiveness, or did you approach it with an open, constructive attitude? By regularly engaging in such reflections, you deepen your understanding of your emotional patterns and learn to guide them more consciously.

The role of adversity in Stoic practice cannot be overstated—it is considered essential for personal growth and strengthening of character. Stoics view adversity as a form of training; just as a runner gains endurance by pushing through physical discomfort, so too can we enhance our emotional resilience by facing and reflecting on life's challenges. This perspective encourages you to see obstacles not as impediments to your happiness but as opportunities to practice virtue and strengthen your spirit. It's not the hardship itself that is valuable, but the way in which you engage with it, applying Stoic Wisdom to emerge stronger and more capable.

Historical and contemporary figures provide compelling case studies of Stoic resilience in action. Consider the example of Nelson Mandela, who, during his 27 years in prison, practiced a form of Stoic resilience by maintaining rigorous self-discipline and using the time for deep reflection and planning. Despite the harsh conditions, Mandela focused on what he could control—his mind and spirit— and emerged as a pivotal leader, embodying Stoic virtues such as endurance, dignity, and forgiveness. In a modern context, consider the CEOs and leaders who navigate the volatile ups and downs of the business world. Those who employ Stoic practices tend to approach crises not just as challenges to survive but as opportunities to refine their strategies and leadership qualities. They use Stoic reflection to assess both their successes and failures, learning from each experience to guide their future actions more wisely.

These reflections and the cultivation of resilience they foster are not just about personal survival or success; they are about contributing to the world with greater strength and wisdom. As you integrate these practices into your daily life, you build not only your capacity to overcome personal challenges but also your ability to impact those around you positively. This chapter has explored how Stoic tools—simplified decision-making frameworks, morning routines focused on serenity, and strategies for handling workplace challenges—can be practically applied to foster resilience and wisdom in everyday life. As we continue, remember that each Stoic practice is a step toward not simply surviving in the world but thriving within it, armed with virtue and resilience.

In sum, this chapter underscores the transformative power of Stoic reflection in building emotional resilience. By embracing reflective practices, understanding the constructive role of adversity, and learning from both historical and contemporary examples, you are equipping yourself with the tools to navigate life's challenges with grace and strength. As we move forward, these principles will continue to guide us, proving that Stoicism is not merely a philosophy of ancient times but a vibrant, living guide for anyone seeking a more fulfilled and resilient life.

4

THE DICHOTOMY OF CONTROL

I n the intricate dance of life, where we constantly juggle our desires, responsibilities, and dreams against the backdrop of a world that often seems chaotic and unpredictable, how do we find our footing? The Stoic philosophy offers a profound and practical guideline known as the Dichotomy of Control. Understanding and applying this principle can not only transform how you navigate challenges but also deepen your sense of peace and empowerment. Let's explore this foundational concept of Stoicism, unravel common misconceptions, and discover how embracing what we can control—and letting go of what we cannot—can lead to a profoundly effective and fulfilling life.

UNDERSTANDING WHAT YOU CAN AND CANNOT CONTROL

At the heart of Stoic Wisdom is the recognition of a simple yet life-changing truth: some things in life are within our control, and many are not. This understanding is crucial because it directly influences our emotional and psychological landscape. The Stoics teach us that our actions, beliefs, and responses are within our sphere of control. In contrast, external events—the actions of other people, the thoughts they harbor, and the myriad circumstances that unfold around us—lie outside this sphere.

Consider the frustration of being stuck in a traffic jam, an event that is clearly beyond your control. The stress and irritation that often accompany such situations aren't caused by the traffic but by our reaction to it. Here, Stoicism offers a liberating perspective: while you cannot control the traffic, you can control your response. Instead of succumbing to frustration, you might choose to listen to an audiobook, reflect on your day, or enjoy some rare solitude. This shift in focus—from the uncontrollable to the controllable—is the key to maintaining tranquility.

However, this principle is often misunderstood. A common misconception is the belief that with enough effort, one can control external outcomes. This misunderstanding can lead to significant frustration and exhaustion because it sets us up for failure when, inevitably, the world does not conform to our will. Stoicism teaches us to invest our energy wisely, focusing on our actions and attitudes, which are ours to command.

Highlighting the Importance of Acceptance

Another critical aspect of the Dichotomy of Control is acceptance—accepting that we cannot control everything. This acceptance is not about resignation but about recognizing reality as it is. By accepting the limits of our control, we avoid wasting energy on pointless resistance and instead devote ourselves to actions that can genuinely make a difference. This acceptance also fosters peace of mind; when we stop fighting against the uncontrollable, we can find serenity even during life's storms.

The power of this principle extends beyond individual peace to interpersonal relationships and professional environments. In the workplace, for example, you might encounter situations where colleagues make decisions that affect you yet are outside your control. Here, Stoicism advises focusing on your response: advocating calmly for your interests, preparing for various outcomes, and finding ways to adapt constructively.

The Dichotomy of Control, therefore, is not just a philosophical statement but a practical strategy for living more effectively. It teaches us to navigate life not by attempting to control the uncontrollable but by mastering what is genuinely ours: our actions, our responses, and our decisions. This mastery leads to a more empowered and effective life, marked not by a lack of challenges but by our skillful and serene navigation through them.

PRACTICAL EXERCISES TO ENHANCE AWARENESS OF CONTROL

Incorporating Stoic principles into your daily life can significantly enhance your ability to distinguish between what you can and cannot control, fostering a more profound sense of peace and effectiveness. To cultivate this awareness, I recommend integrating specific, straightforward exercises into your routine. These practices, designed to sharpen your recognition of control, help you to focus your energies more wisely and respond to life's unpredictabilities with composure and insight.

One such practice is daily journaling, a method that not only aids in reflection but also the practical application of Stoic principles. Each evening, dedicate a few minutes to jot down the day's events, categorizing them under 'controllable' and 'uncontrollable.' For instance, you might note a heated discussion with a colleague under 'uncontrollable,' as their reactions are not within your power.

Conversely, your choice to remain calm or to engage respectfully can be noted under 'controllable'. This simple act of categorization helps to internalize the dichotomy of control, gradually shifting your focus from external circumstances to your internal responses. Over time, this practice can transform your approach to challenges, leading you to a more proactive and centered engagement with life.

Mindfulness practices also play a crucial role in enhancing awareness of control. Mindfulness involves maintaining a moment-by-moment awareness of our thoughts, feelings, bodily sensations, and surrounding environment. By cultivating mindfulness, you develop the ability to observe your reactions to situations without immediately acting on them. This pause is crucial; it provides the space to assess whether you are trying to control the uncontrollable. Regular mindfulness meditation can be particularly effective. Dedicate a few minutes each day to sit quietly and focus on your breath. When thoughts or worries arise, gently acknowledge them and assess whether they concern things within your control. If not, visualize setting them aside, focusing instead on your breathing and the present moment. This practice not only reduces stress but also reinforces the Stoic discipline of focusing on the present and what you can influence.

Developing a 'Control Checklist'

To further this awareness, I suggest creating a 'control checklist,' a simple yet powerful tool to use in real-time situations. This checklist should include questions like: "Can I control this situation?", "What aspects can I influence?" and "Am I focusing on my reaction or trying to control the outcome?" Keep this checklist accessible—perhaps on a small card in your wallet or as a note on your phone. In moments of stress or decision, run through this checklist to realign your focus toward what you can effectively manage. This practice not only saves you from unnecessary frustration but also enhances your decision-making and problem-solving abilities by keeping your energy directed toward actionable areas.

Using Scenarios for Practice

To solidify your understanding and application of the dichotomy of control, consider setting aside time each week to analyze and discuss specific scenarios, either on your own or with a group. For example, imagine you are planning a special family event, and the weather forecast suddenly predicts rain. Explore how you might apply the dichotomy of control here. You cannot control the weather, but you can control your preparations, such as arranging for indoor alternatives or providing umbrellas for guests. By discussing and dissecting such scenarios, you can refine your ability to distinguish between controllable and uncontrollable elements, enhancing your adaptability and resourcefulness in real-life situations.

Through these exercises—journaling, mindfulness, the control checklist, and scenario analysis—you equip yourself with practical tools to embody Stoic Wisdom in your daily life. These practices not only deepen your philosophical understanding but also enhance your practical skills in managing life's uncertainties with grace and effectiveness. In doing so, you cultivate a life not just of survival but of success, characterized by an empowered serenity and a proactive engagement with the world.

LETTING GO OF ANXIETY OVER THE UNCONTROLLABLE

In our quest for control over our lives, we often find ourselves ensnared by anxiety—an emotional response that not only disrupts our harmony but can significantly hinder our ability to enjoy life and perform effectively. This anxiety frequently stems from a deep-seated desire to control what is fundamentally uncontrollable. Understanding this relationship between control and anxiety is the first step toward alleviating the latter, and Stoicism provides a valuable framework for this understanding.

Anxiety often arises when we face situations that remind us of our limitations—events or outcomes that we cannot predict or control, such as the health of a loved one, the stability of our job, or the state of global affairs. The Stoic approach teaches us that this anxiety is not a direct result of the situations themselves but from our perceptions and the unrealistic expectation that we should be able to control these external factors. Recognizing that some aspects of life are simply beyond our control can significantly reduce the anxiety associated with them. This recognition frees us from the burden of trying to control the uncontrollable and directs our efforts towards areas where we can actually make a difference—in our attitudes and responses.

Cognitive reframing techniques can be particularly effective in aiding in this transformation of perspective. These techniques involve altering your mental approach to a situation and changing your emotional response in the process. For instance, instead of viewing a looming project deadline as a stress-inducing demand, reframe it as an opportunity to showcase your skills and dedication. Similarly, if worrying about a family member's health, reframe your concern into proactive engagement—such as encouraging healthier lifestyle choices or supporting medical appointments. By reframing these situations, you shift from a passive state of worry about uncontrollable outcomes to an active state of engagement with controllable actions, thereby reducing anxiety and increasing effectiveness.

Another powerful practice to lower anxiety is to establish a routine of relinquishment—a dedicated time to consciously let go of the things outside your control. This could be a daily or weekly session where you reflect on the events or worries occupying your mind and categorically release those that you cannot influence. For example, you might write down your concerns and physically mark those that are beyond your control, symbolically setting them aside. Documenting the emotional impact of this practice can be enlightening; many find that this routine not only clarifies what is within their control but also brings a profound sense of relief and lightness as the burden of unnecessary worries is lifted.

The effectiveness of these strategies is not just theoretical but is supported by numerous success stories. Take the case of a corporate lawyer who struggled with chronic anxiety about case outcomes, client reactions, and courtroom performances—factors that were often unpredictable and beyond her direct control. By applying Stoic principles and engaging in cognitive reframing and routine relinquishment, she learned to focus on her preparation and effort— the aspects she could control. Over time, not only did her anxiety diminish, but her performance improved, as she was able to devote more energy to her legal strategies and client consultations rather than wasting it on unproductive worry.

In another example, a school principal used Stoicism to manage his anxiety over educational policy changes—a largely uncontrollable aspect of his job. Through regular reframing exercises, he began to see these changes not as threats but as challenges to his ability to adapt and innovate. His routine of relinquishment involved writing down his fears about policy impacts and formally setting aside time to consider practical responses rather than dwelling on potential negatives. This approach not only reduced his stress but also made him a more proactive and respected leader in his educational community.

These stories highlight a fundamental truth in Stoic philosophy: often, the control we seek is not over external events but over our own internal states. By focusing on what we can control—our responses, our mindset, our actions—we can significantly reduce our anxiety and navigate life with greater calm and confidence. This Stoic practice of focusing on the controllable, reframing our perceptions, and consciously letting go of the rest can transform not only how we handle challenges but also how we live our lives—more engaged with the present, more at peace with the uncontrollable, and more empowered in our daily actions.

HOW EMBRACING LACK OF CONTROL CAN LEAD TO GREATER HAPPINESS

In the maze of life's challenges, the act of surrendering control over external events can seem counterintuitive. Yet, it is within this paradox of surrender that a profound transformation can occur, leading to a greater sense of personal power and happiness. Stoicism teaches us that by releasing our tight grip on the illusion of control, we open ourselves to a more harmonious and joyful experience of life. Embracing what we cannot control does not diminish our power; instead, it redirects our energies towards what truly matters —our responses, our values, and our growth.

This surrender is not about giving up action but about redefining where we place our efforts and trust. It involves a deep faith in the process of life, believing that even in chaos, there is a pattern that will emerge, a lesson to be learned, and growth to be experienced. Trusting this process means having faith in our own capabilities to adapt and find meaning, regardless of circumstances. This faith is crucial, for it is what allows us to face uncertainty with courage rather than fear. It anchors us in the belief that whatever the outcome, we have the resilience and the wisdom to navigate through it.

Consider the natural world, which thrives on a balance of control and surrender. A tree does not try to control the wind, the rain, or the sun; it simply grows, adapts, and thrives in the midst of these uncontrollable forces. Similarly, when we embrace the uncontrollable aspects of our lives with grace, we tap into a more profound source of happiness and peace. Engaging with community and nature serves as a powerful reminder of this balance. By being part of a community, whether participating in local events, volunteering, or simply connecting with neighbors, we reinforce the notion that we are part of something larger than ourselves. This involvement can alleviate the pressure of feeling that everything is up to us, offering comfort and support through collective endeavors.

Historical and philosophical anecdotes abound with figures who have embraced the limits of their control and found profound happiness. The philosopher Socrates, for instance, exhibited remarkable tranquility and humor in the face of his unjust execution, a fate he did not control and could not avoid. His acceptance of his fate, rooted in a life spent pursuing virtue and wisdom, turned his final moments into a lasting testament to the power of inner freedom. Similarly, the modern example of Viktor Frankl, who survived the horrors of a concentration camp, shows us that even in extreme conditions, our attitudes and responses hold the key to our freedom and happiness. Frankl's philosophy, that one could find meaning and personal growth in every moment of existence, no matter how brutal, provides a modern-day echo of Stoic resilience and joy in the face of life's uncontrollability.

As you reflect on these ideas, consider how you might start to relinquish the need for control in your life. Perhaps it begins with a simple daily affirmation, acknowledging what you can and cannot control, or maybe it involves a more active engagement with the community or nature. Whatever form it takes, the practice of embracing the uncontrollable not only enhances your well-being but also enriches your interactions with the world around you. By surrendering control where it cannot be actually exerted, you gain a better command over your own life, navigating your experiences with an empowered serenity and a joyful heart.

In the journey through the pages of this book, we have explored not only the theoretical underpinnings of Stoicism but also its practical applications, from understanding the dichotomy of control to embracing the paradox of surrender. These principles, woven into the fabric of daily life, offer a robust framework for dealing with the complexities of modern existence. As we move forward, remember that the essence of Stoic Wisdom lies not merely in enduring life's challenges but in transforming them into avenues for personal growth and fulfillment.

In the next chapter, we will delve deeper into the Stoic practices that can help you cultivate resilience and inner peace, ensuring that you are not just surviving but thriving, no matter what life throws your way. This journey of exploration and application continues to unfold, offering ever more profound insights into how Stoicism can illuminate and enrich your life path.

5

RELATIONSHIPS THROUGH A STOIC LENS

Navigating the intricate webs of relationships, be it with friends, family, or colleagues, can often feel like trying to sail in turbulent waters. Conflicts arise, and under the force of emotional winds, our reactions might steer us away from the tranquil harbors we aim for. But what if you could equip yourself with the philosophical compass of Stoicism, guiding you to navigate these interactions with poise and understanding? Stoicism, with its profound insights into human behavior and emotion, provides invaluable tools for managing relationships in a way that not only preserves but enriches them.

THE STOIC'S GUIDE TO HANDLING CONFLICT IN RELATIONSHIPS

Conflicts in relationships often spring from misaligned perceptions. Each person views the world through their own lens, colored by individual experiences, emotions, and expectations. Stoicism teaches us that these differing perceptions are a fundamental aspect of human nature and that recognizing this can significantly de-escalate potential tensions. When you acknowledge that another's viewpoint is merely their perception of reality, not an objective truth, you open the door to understanding and reconciliation rather than conflict.

To cultivate this understanding, Stoicism encourages the practice of empathy and perspective-taking. Imagine stepping into the shoes of another, seeing through their eyes, and feeling with their heart. This exercise does not just broaden your understanding of their actions and reactions; it fosters a deeper connection, a vital element in building and sustaining harmonious relationships. For instance, if a friend reacts angrily to a canceled plan, instead of mirroring their frustration, try to understand the underlying feelings. Perhaps they had been looking forward to this as a much-needed break in a stressful week. Recognizing this can shift your response from one of irritation to one of compassion, paving the way for a calm and constructive conversation.

Implementing Stoic calm in heated moments is another powerful strategy. Stoicism doesn't teach suppression of emotion but rather the management of it. One effective technique is the pause—a deliberate cessation of immediate reaction. When a conflict arises, instead of responding in the heat of the moment, take a deep breath or even step away if necessary. This pause gives you the space to collect your thoughts, temper your emotions, and approach the situation with a level head. By responding rather than reacting, you embody the Stoic ideal of self-control, turning potential arguments into opportunities for open and productive dialogues.

Moreover, Stoicism provides Wisdom in choosing your battles wisely. Not every disagreement demands your energy, and not every conflict merits confrontation. Some issues, when viewed through the lens of Stoic discernment, reveal themselves to be minor or based on quickly resolved misunderstandings. Stoicism teaches us to focus on what truly matters—such as respect, understanding, and love. Before engaging in or escalating a conflict, ask yourself whether this issue will matter in the long run or if it's merely a distraction from the health and happiness of your relationship. Often, you'll find that letting go of minor grievances can lead to greater peace and stability in your relationships.

Exercise: Reflective Journaling on Relationship Conflicts

Consider keeping a reflective journal where you document and analyze conflicts that arise in your relationships. For each conflict, write down:

- The perceived cause of the conflict.
- Your initial emotional response.
- How you chose to handle the situation.
- The outcome of the conflict.
- Lessons learned and how you might handle a similar situation in the future.

This practice not only aids in self-reflection but also helps in developing a more Stoic approach to handling relationship conflicts, focusing on understanding, empathy, and the essential virtues that strengthen bonds.

By embracing these Stoic practices, you equip yourself with the tools to handle conflicts not just with effectiveness but with a grace that enriches your connections with others. These strategies, grounded in ancient wisdom, are profoundly relevant in our modern lives, helping to transform potential discord into opportunities for deeper understanding and stronger relationships. As you continue to apply these teachings, you may find that the Stoic approach not only resolves conflicts but also prevents them, fostering an atmosphere of mutual respect and peace in all your interpersonal engagements.

LOVE AND STOICISM: MAINTAINING INDIVIDUALITY AND HARMONY

In the delicate dance of relationships, especially those tinged with romance, the balance between emotional investment and maintaining rational independence is often a tightrope walk. Stoicism provides insightful guidance on navigating this balance with its deep roots in understanding the nature of emotions and human interactions. The Stoic practice of caring deeply for others while sustaining an inner detachment is not about emotional coldness, but rather about protecting one's peace of mind. This approach helps maintain clarity and composure, allowing you to love freely without becoming overly dependent on the reciprocation or behavior of your partner.

This detachment is crucial in preserving your well-being in relationships. It involves seeing and appreciating your partner for who they are but also recognizing that your emotional state does not need to be entirely contingent upon their actions or moods. For instance, if a partner is going through a rough patch and becomes distant, a Stoic approach would be to offer support without feeling personally slighted or overly distressed. This balanced attitude helps you remain supportive and present yet emotionally stable, whether the relationship is flourishing or facing challenges.

Cultivating self-sufficiency in relationships is another cornerstone of Stoic practice. It encourages you to find sources of happiness and fulfillment from within yourself rather than relying solely on your partner or friends. This self-sufficiency is about developing your hobbies, interests, and emotional resilience. Engaging in activities that fulfill you independently of your relationship not only reduces the pressure on your partner to be your sole source of happiness but also leads to a healthier, more balanced relationship. For example, pursuing a personal hobby or career ambition can provide a sense of accomplishment and satisfaction that complements the joys found in your relationship rather than competing with it.

Harmonizing personal growth with relational growth is an essential aspect of Stoic love. Stoicism teaches that personal virtues such as wisdom, courage, and temperance can greatly enhance relationships. Conversely, healthy relationships can foster personal growth, creating a virtuous cycle. This mutual support is about encouraging each other to pursue individual goals and qualities, not in a spirit of competition but in one of collaboration. For instance, practicing temperance might help you manage emotional reactions within your relationship, while your relationship might provide opportunities to practice and reinforce this feature through real-life challenges and interactions.

This synergy between personal and relational growth is encapsulated beautifully in the Stoic idea that love should be based on the admiration of each other's qualities. Stoic love is not merely an emotional affection but a profound connection that inspires both parties to strive towards a life of mutual benefit. In a Stoic relationship, partners motivate each other to be their best selves, not through criticism or control but through example and mutual support. This type of relationship is deeply fulfilling because it is based not just on emotional attachment but on a shared commitment to living virtuously.

By integrating these Stoic principles into your relationships, you cultivate not only a deeper connection with your partner but also a more profound understanding and application of Stoicism in your life. This approach to relationships offers a pathway to true companionship, where love is expressed not just in words or emotions but through a shared journey towards virtue and fulfillment. Through this lens, every interaction in your relationship becomes an opportunity to practice and reinforce Stoic principles, enriching both your life and that of your partner.

EFFECTIVE COMMUNICATION STRATEGIES INSPIRED BY STOICISM

In the realm of human interactions, the art of communication is paramount. Stoicism, with its profound emphasis on integrity and rationality, provides a robust framework for enhancing how we express ourselves and connect with others. Promoting transparent and honest communication is foundational in Stoic practice, reflecting the virtue of integrity. When you engage in conversations, whether they are casual chats or significant discussions, being honest and sincere not only fosters trust but also builds a solid foundation for meaningful relationships. This transparency means being open about your thoughts and feelings but also being candid about your limitations and uncertainties. For instance, in a professional setting, rather than agreeing to a deadline you know is unrealistic, a Stoic approach would be to express your concerns honestly and negotiate a more feasible timeline, which not only ensures you can deliver quality work but also establishes your reliability and respect for truth.

Moreover, Stoicism teaches the importance of listening—a skill that is often overshadowed by the urge to speak and be heard. Authentic listening, from a Stoic perspective, isn't just about hearing the words that others say but involves a deeper level of engagement. It's about tuning into the emotions and intentions behind those words. This form of empathetic listening can transform interactions, making the person you're communicating with genuinely feel understood and valued. It involves an active effort to see the world from the other person's perspective, which not only enriches your understanding but can also diffuse potential conflicts before they escalate. For example, if a friend seems upset over a seemingly trivial matter, carefully listening might reveal underlying issues such as stress or insecurity that are the true roots of their distress. By responding to these deeper issues rather than the surface symptoms, you can provide support that is genuinely effective and appreciated.

The realm of non-verbal communication also holds substantial weight in Stoic practice. Stoics understand that much of what we communicate is not transmitted through words but through our body language, facial expressions, and even our silence. Being mindful of non-verbal cues can provide critical insights into others' thoughts and feelings, often revealing more than their words might convey. For instance, a colleague might say they agree with a decision, but their crossed arms and averted gaze might suggest otherwise. Observing these signs enables you to address concerns that haven't been explicitly stated, fostering an atmosphere of openness and trust. Furthermore, being conscious of your own non-verbal signals can help you communicate more effectively. A calm demeanor and open posture can convey confidence and receptivity, encouraging others to engage more openly with you.

Lastly, Stoicism advocates for a balanced expression of assertiveness and kindness—a combination that is particularly powerful in communication. Being assertive means expressing your needs and boundaries clearly and confidently, without passivity or aggression. This assertiveness, tempered with kindness, aligns with Stoic principles of courage and justice, ensuring that your communications not only respect your values but also consider the well-being of others. For example, if you feel overwhelmed by your workload, expressing this to your supervisor assertively yet respectfully can lead to a more manageable allocation of tasks. Similarly, if a friend repeatedly cancels plans at the last minute, addressing the issue directly yet kindly can lead to a discussion about respect and reliability in your relationship.

These strategies—promoting honesty, practicing empathetic listening, observing non-verbal cues, and combining assertiveness with kindness—are not just techniques but reflections of deeper Stoic values. They are about respecting yourself and others, striving for harmony and understanding, and navigating complex human relationships with wisdom and grace. As you continue to integrate these Stoic principles into your communication practices, you will likely find that not only do your interactions become more effective and satisfying, but they also become more enriching, reflecting the profound Stoic pursuit of living a virtuous and meaningful life.

FORGIVENESS AND LETTING GO: A STOIC APPROACH

Forgiveness in the realm of Stoicism is not merely about absolving others but is more profoundly about restoring one's peace of mind— seen as a release of resentment and a pathway back to emotional equilibrium. The Stoics believed that harboring resentment ties us to the past, a realm over which we have no control and which distracts us from the present moment where our power truly lies. Forgiveness, therefore, is fundamentally about reclaiming control over our emotional well-being by letting go of grievances that cloud our tranquility.

This process begins with understanding the inherent flaws and frailties that are part of being human. Recognizing that everyone, including ourselves, is capable of making mistakes or acting out of ignorance, fear, or distress can change the emotional landscape from one of anger to one of empathy. This shift is crucial because it allows us to see the situation from a broader perspective where our personal hurt does not obscure our capacity for compassion. For instance, if a colleague's harsh words during a stressful project upset you, understanding their pressure and anxiety can help mitigate your hurt feelings and lead you toward forgiveness.

Practically, forgiveness involves a series of intentional steps. The first step is to clearly acknowledge the hurt or damage done rather than denying or diminishing it. This acknowledgment is vital as it validates your feelings and defines what exactly needs to be forgiven. Following this, engage in a deliberate decision-making process where you choose to let go of the resentment. This might involve writing a letter of forgiveness (which you do not necessarily have to send) or simply saying out loud to yourself that you choose to forgive. The act of deciding to forgive is empowering—it shifts the situation from something that happens to you to something you control.

Next, actively work on releasing the emotional charge connected to the memory of the offense. This could be through meditation, where you visualize letting go of the resentment, or through physical activity like running or yoga, where you imagine releasing the negative feelings with each breath or movement. Over time, these practices can diminish the emotional weight of past grievances, helping to restore your inner peace.

The benefits of practicing forgiveness are profound and complex. On a personal level, letting go of grudges can lead to decreased anxiety, lower blood pressure, and overall improved mental health. These changes occur because forgiveness reduces the physiological burden that anger and resentment place on the body. Emotionally, forgiving others can lead to heightened feelings of happiness and contentment as you reclaim the energy previously consumed by negative emotions. Relationally, forgiveness can transform dynamics, paving the way for healthier and more understanding interactions. It removes the barriers of bitterness and allows for the possibility of rebuilding trust and empathy, essential components for robust relationships.

In Stoicism, the act of forgiveness is not just an occasional remedy for grievances but a regular practice that maintains and restores peace. It aligns perfectly with the Stoic endeavor to live a virtuous life, for it requires and nurtures virtues like courage, justice, temperance, and wisdom. Each act of forgiveness is both a practice of these virtues and a step towards a more profound, more peaceful, and more resilient life.

As we culminate this exploration of relationships through a Stoic lens, we've traversed the terrain of conflict management, the balancing act in love, effective communication, and the freeing act of forgiveness. Each of these facets, enriched by Stoic Wisdom, invites you to engage more deeply, more serenely, and more meaningfully in your relationships. The next chapter will delve into managing emotions and personal growth, continuing to build on the solid foundation of Stoic practices we've established thus far. Here, we will explore how Stoicism not only helps in navigating external challenges but also profoundly transforms our internal landscape.

6

MANAGING EMOTIONS AND GROWTH

I n the rich tapestry of human experience, emotions weave vibrant, often tumultuous patterns, influencing everything from our daily interactions to our most profound life decisions. This chapter delves into the Stoic approach to managing emotions, particularly focusing on anger and frustration—emotions that, if left unchecked, can disrupt our peace and hinder our growth. Here, you'll learn not only to understand these powerful feelings but also to manage them with wisdom and grace, using Stoic practices that have stood the test of time.

STOIC PRACTICES TO CURB ANGER AND FRUSTRATION

Understanding the Triggers and Responses

Anger, often seen as a destructive force, can actually serve as a signal, pointing us toward unresolved issues or unmet expectations. The first step in managing anger is to recognize what triggers it. These triggers can be as varied as feeling undervalued at work, facing disrespect in a relationship, or dealing with the chronic stress of daily commutes. Once recognized, it's crucial to observe how this anger manifests in your thoughts and behaviors—do you withdraw silently or lash out verbally? Understanding these patterns is critical to addressing the root causes and reshaping your responses.

Implementing the Stoic Pause and Reflect Technique

The Stoic pause is a powerful tool in your emotional arsenal. When you feel anger rising, give yourself the gift of time—just a few seconds can transform your reaction. During this pause, engage in reflective questioning: "What is truly causing my anger? Is my response going to be beneficial or detrimental? What would a wise person do in my position?" This moment of introspection can shift your perspective from a knee-jerk reaction to a considered response, allowing you to address the issue with composure and clarity.

Applying the Principle of Impermanence

Stoicism teaches us that all external events are transient—they come and go. By internalizing this principle of impermanence, you can lessen the intensity of your anger. For instance, if you are infuriated by a project setback, remind yourself that this situation is temporary and will soon be just a memory. This broader perspective reduces the emotional weight of the event, helping you approach it with a balanced mindset and focus on constructive solutions rather than getting bogged down by frustration.

Encouraging the Adoption of Empathy

Expanding your perspective to include the intentions and circumstances of others can significantly reduce feelings of anger and lead to more compassionate responses. When someone acts in a way that triggers your anger, try to understand their motives and background. Perhaps they are under stress or unaware of the impact of their actions. By practicing empathy, you not only mitigate your anger but also open up pathways for more transparent communication and more effective conflict resolution.

Interactive Element: Reflective Journaling Exercise

To integrate these Stoic practices into your daily life, maintain a reflective journal. Each night, jot down instances where you felt anger or frustration during the day. Describe the trigger, your initial reaction, and how you applied Stoic techniques to handle the situation. Reflect on what worked and what could be improved. This exercise not only solidifies your learning but also tracks your progress over time, enhancing your ability to manage these challenging emotions with increasing skill and wisdom.

Through these Stoic practices—understanding triggers, pausing to reflect, recognizing impermanence, and practicing empathy—you can transform your approach to anger and frustration. Instead of being overwhelmed by these emotions, you learn to handle them with grace and effectiveness, using them as tools for personal growth and better relationships. As we continue to explore the vast landscape of handling emotions through Stoicism, remember that each step you take is not just about controlling feelings but about cultivating a deeper, more resilient version of yourself, ready to face the world with confidence and composure.

TURNING ENVY AND JEALOUSY INTO MOTIVATORS WITH STOICISM

Envy and jealousy, if left unchecked, can erode our inner peace and cloud our perceptions of our own lives. Yet, viewed through the lens of Stoicism, these emotions can serve as valuable tools for self-reflection and personal growth. Rather than allowing these feelings to foster resentment, you can transform them into catalysts for enhancing your own life and achieving genuine fulfillment. This transformative approach involves redefining success, utilizing envy as a reflective tool, cultivating an abundance mindset, and turning jealousy into a motivational force.

Redefining Personal Success

In our society, success is often measured by external benchmarks: career achievements, material acquisitions, or social status. However, Stoicism invites you to redefine success based on internal virtues and personal excellence. This internal measure focuses not on comparing yourself to others but on assessing your growth and integrity. Ask yourself: "Am I more patient, kind, and wise than I was last year?" By shifting the focus from external validation to internal development, you not only foster self-contentment but also insulate yourself from the destabilizing effects of envy. When you know your worth and your goals are aligned with your deepest values, the achievements of others become less a source of jealousy and more a reminder of the many paths to personal excellence.

Using Envy as a Mirror

When feelings of envy arise, instead of pushing them away or letting them sour your mood, use them as mirrors to reflect on your desires and aspirations. What is it about someone else's situation that triggers your envy? Is it their professional success, their relationships, or perhaps their lifestyle? These reflections can reveal essential truths about what you value and what might be missing or unfulfilled in your own life. Instead of resenting others' successes, analyze these feelings to understand better what changes you might pursue in your own life to achieve fulfillment. This introspective process not only diminishes envy but also clarifies your goals, steering you toward a more authentic and satisfying life path.

Developing a Mindset of Abundance

One of the most effective antidotes to envy and jealousy is cultivating an abundance mindset. This perspective focuses on appreciating what you already have rather than fixating on what others possess. Begin by regularly counting your blessings—acknowledge your talents, cherish your relationships, and celebrate your progress, no matter how small. Practicing gratitude shifts your focus from scarcity to abundance, reducing feelings of envy and increasing life satisfaction. When you view life as plentiful and opportunities as abundant, the success of others ceases to be a threat and instead becomes a source of inspiration.

Transforming Envy into Motivation

Finally, transform feelings of envy and jealousy into motivation to improve yourself. If a colleague's promotion sparks envy, let it motivate you to develop your skills or to take on new projects. If a friend's fitness achievements stir jealousy, use that as inspiration to prioritize your own health and wellness goals. By channeling your emotional energy positively, you not only overcome detrimental feelings but also propel yourself toward personal growth and success. This proactive approach not only enhances your well-being but also turns potentially negative emotions into stepping stones for self-improvement.

Through these practices, you can transform envy and jealousy from sources of distress into instruments of personal empowerment. By redefining success, using envy as a mirror for reflection, cultivating an abundance mindset, and converting jealousy into motivation, you align more closely with Stoic principles, leading a life driven not by comparison and resentment but by self-improvement and contentment. As you continue to apply these strategies, remember that the path to personal excellence is not about surpassing others but about surpassing your previous self, achieving a state of fulfillment that is both deeply personal and profoundly rewarding.

OVERCOMING FEAR WITH COURAGE AND RATIONAL THOUGHT

Fear, a primal human emotion, serves both as a protector and a barrier. While it can preserve us from real dangers, it often also stands as an obstacle to personal growth and fulfillment. Stoicism, with its emphasis on rationality and self-control, provides valuable tools for dissecting and managing fears, transforming them from ambiguous shadows that haunt our minds into clear challenges that we can confront and overcome. This section aims to guide you through understanding your fears, strengthening your rational thinking, cultivating authentic Stoic courage, and adopting practices such as controlled exposure to face and conquer your anxieties effectively.

Identifying Irrational Fears

First, let's differentiate between rational and irrational fears. Rational fears are those that have a factual basis in danger; for instance, the fear of touching a hot stove, which protects us from burns. Irrational fears, however, do not have a direct correlation to imminent danger. These might include fears of public speaking, heights, or even initiating personal relationships. The Stoic approach encourages us to challenge our fears by examining their validity. Ask yourself: "What is the evidence for this fear? Is there a real threat to my well-being, or is it a perceived danger?" By scrutinizing your fears under the light of reason, you can often reveal that many anxieties are not supported by reality and are instead constructs of our minds.

Strengthening Rational Thinking

Stoicism teaches us to strengthen our rational thinking to combat irrational fears, which involves systematically evaluating the worst-case scenarios of feared situations and then realistically assessing the probability of these outcomes. For example, if you're afraid of failing an important exam, consider the actual consequences: you might need to retake the test or review the material more thoroughly. When viewed rationally, the ultimate consequences are often not as catastrophic as our fears would lead us to believe. This methodical evaluation helps to minimize the perceived impact of the fear, making it more manageable and less intimidating.

Cultivating Stoic Courage

Stoic courage is not merely the absence of fear but the resolve to act rightly and virtuously despite fear's presence. It involves recognizing that genuine harm comes not from external circumstances but from failing to live according to our values. To cultivate Stoic courage, start by affirming your commitment to act with integrity, regardless of personal fears. When faced with a situation that triggers fear, remind yourself of your core values and the importance of upholding them. This focus shifts your perspective from avoiding fear to acting meaningfully despite it, empowering you to take action aligned with your principles.

Practice Exposure Therapy

One practical method to manage fear is through controlled exposure, a technique aligned with Stoic confrontational practices. This approach involves gradually and repeatedly exposing yourself to the object of your fear in a controlled, safe manner. If you're afraid of public speaking, for instance, you might start by speaking to a small, supportive group and gradually increase the audience size as your confidence grows. Over time, this repeated exposure reduces the emotional response associated with the fear, desensitizing you to the anxiety it used to provoke. This practice not only lessens the fear itself but also builds your confidence and proficiency in the previously feared activity.

By applying these Stoic strategies—identifying irrational fears, strengthening rational thinking, cultivating courage, and practicing controlled exposure—you can transform your approach to fear from one of avoidance to one of engagement. These methods encourage not merely the management of fear but its mastery, enabling you to live more freely and fully, unencumbered by irrational anxieties. As you continue to implement these practices, you may find that the fears which once seemed insurmountable become sources of strength and growth, each conquered fear adding to your resilience and zest for life.

THE ROLE OF REFLECTION IN PERSONAL STOIC GROWTH

Reflection is a cornerstone of Stoic practice, serving not just as a method for self-improvement but as a daily ritual that aligns your life more closely with the core virtues of Stoicism—wisdom, justice, courage, and temperance. By integrating the practice of daily reflection, you engage in a thoughtful examination of your thoughts, decisions, and actions, which illuminates patterns in your behavior that may be invisible during the rush of daily activities. This process allows you to pause and consider not only what you did and why you did it but also how you can improve and align your actions more closely with Stoic principles.

Imagine ending each day by sitting quietly and reviewing the events and interactions of your day. Consider the moments when you felt proud of your actions, but also those when you fell short of your Stoic ideals. Perhaps you reacted hastily to a comment from a coworker, or maybe you missed an opportunity to help a friend in need. Reflecting on these moments encourages a deeper understanding of your personal values and how effectively you are embodying them. This practice isn't about self-criticism but about self-awareness and growth—it helps you recognize your strengths and identify areas where you can develop greater virtue and resilience.

In addition to daily reflection, starting a reflective writing practice can significantly enhance your journey of personal growth. Keeping a Stoic journal allows you to record not just the events of each day but also your emotional and intellectual responses to those events. This kind of writing provides a space to explore your thoughts and feelings more deeply, to question your assumptions, and to plan how you might better handle similar situations in the future. For instance, if you find that certain events consistently trigger negative emotions, writing about them can help you understand and eventually master them. Over time, this journal becomes not just a record of your life but a roadmap of your personal evolution, showing you how far you have come and where you still wish to go.

Reflection also plays a crucial role in helping you detach emotionally from intense situations and is key to maintaining clarity and making wise decisions. Stoicism teaches that we should strive to respond to events with rationality rather than emotion. By reflecting on our experiences, particularly those that elicit strong emotional reactions, we can begin to see these situations more objectively. This detachment doesn't mean ignoring your emotions but rather understanding them as natural responses that do not have to dictate your actions. For example, if you're upset by a family member's criticism, reflection can help you understand why the criticism hurt and how you can address the underlying issues without damaging the relationship.

The benefits of reflective growth are profound. Regular reflection fosters a greater self-awareness, which is the first step toward self-mastery. It also promotes emotional regulation, helping you maintain your equanimity in challenging situations. Perhaps most importantly, reflection leads to greater wisdom and contentment. By regularly assessing and adjusting your behavior to align with Stoic virtues, you not only become a better person but also find greater satisfaction in your daily life. This satisfaction comes not from external achievements but from knowing that you are living true to your values and continuously striving to improve.

As you incorporate these reflective practices into your life, you will likely find that they not only enhance your personal growth but also enrich your relationships with others. They inspire you to be more mindful and present, both with yourself and with those around you, fostering deeper connections and a more compassionate approach to interpersonal interactions.

In this chapter, we have explored various dimensions of managing emotions and fostering personal growth through Stoicism. From understanding and curbing anger to transforming envy and overcoming fear, each section has provided practical strategies for harnessing your emotions and aligning your actions with Stoic principles. As we move forward, remember that these practices are not just exercises in self-control but pathways to a richer, more meaningful life.

7

STOICISM IN TIMES OF CRISIS

In life, we are invariably confronted by moments that wrench our hearts and twist our paths in unexpected ways. Loss, an inescapable human experience, comes to us all, clothed in various forms—be it the profound grief of losing a loved one, the emptiness following the end of a significant relationship, or the shock and uncertainty stemming from sudden unemployment. How does one find the strength to move forward when weighed down by such profound loss? Here, the ancient wisdom of Stoicism stands as a beacon, offering not only comfort but a powerful framework for transforming our response to loss.

FINDING STRENGTH IN STOIC PHILOSOPHY DURING LOSS

Acknowledging the Impact of Loss

The first step in navigating through loss is acknowledging its impact on our lives. It is a profound, often devastating experience that can disrupt our emotional balance and sense of stability. The pain of loss is real and intense, and Stoicism doesn't ask us to suppress this pain but to face it with courage and clarity. It teaches us that grief, though painful, is a natural response to loss, and accepting this emotion is crucial for healing.

Stoic Views on Attachment and Impermanence

Stoicism offers a unique perspective on attachment and the nature of external things. It teaches that everything around us, including our relationships and careers, is impermanent and subject to change. This might sound disheartening at first, but this recognition is vital for building internal resilience. The Stoic philosophers, such as Marcus Aurelius, remind us that our distress often arises not merely from loss itself but from our mistaken belief that we could possess something—be it a person, position, or phase of life—forever. Understanding and accepting the impermanence of all things can lessen the pain of loss, as it aligns our expectations with the reality of our transient existence.

Encouraging the Use of Stoic Reflections

In the wake of loss, Stoicism encourages the practice of reflection—turning inward to draw strength from the values and experiences we shared with what we have lost. Instead of focusing solely on the void left by the loss, Stoicism teaches us to cherish the memories and lessons learned from the relationship or situation. Reflect on what the lost loved one or job brought into your life—strength, love, growth, or resilience. These reflections are not about holding on to the past but about honoring the impact of these experiences on our personal development.

Promote the Adoption of a Forward-Looking Perspective

Stoicism is inherently forward-looking, emphasizing growth and the potential for personal development even in the face of adversity. It inspires us to shift our focus from what we have lost to the possibilities that lie ahead. This does not mean we forget the past or the pain; instead, we use it as a foundation for building a future enriched by the wisdom gained through our experiences of love and loss. Stoic optimism is not about expecting life to be easy but about recognizing our capacity to endure and grow from our challenges. It propels us to move forward, not despite our losses, but with a deeper appreciation of life's fragility and our strengths.

Reflective Exercise: Envisioning a Path Forward

Consider setting aside some time for a reflective exercise. Visualize your life as a journey with many paths. Some you have already traveled, filled with memories and lessons, while others lie ahead, unexplored and ripe with potential. Reflect on the paths influenced by your loss—what strengths did you gain? What values were highlighted? Now, look forward. Envision yourself walking a new path, carrying forward the wisdom and love from your past experiences. What does this path look like? How does it feel to acknowledge your past but also to embrace the potential of your future? This visualization can help reinforce the Stoic practice of using loss as a stepping stone for growth and renewal.

By integrating these Stoic principles into our lives, we equip ourselves not only to survive the crises of loss but to emerge from them with greater resilience and clarity. Through the practice of Stoic reflection, the acceptance of life's impermanence, and courageously facing our grief, we find the strength to continue our journey with renewed purpose and wisdom. As we move forward, let us carry with us the lessons of Stoicism—not as mere spectators of our fate but as active participants in shaping a life of virtue and meaning, even in the wake of loss.

STOIC STRATEGIES FOR COPING WITH UNEXPECTED CHANGE

Change is as much a part of life's fabric as the seasons that cycle from spring to winter. Stoic philosophy, with its deep roots in understanding and adapting to the impermanence of life, teaches us to view change not as an anomaly but as an inherent aspect of the human experience. This perspective is crucial because it helps prepare us for the inevitable shifts we will encounter, from negligible alterations in our daily routines to significant transformations in our personal and professional lives. By framing change as a natural and expected element of living, Stoicism arms us with the mental and emotional skills needed to face new circumstances with a composed and measured response rather than resistance or fear.

Developing cognitive flexibility is essential in adapting to change effectively. This trait, which involves the ability to adjust one's thinking and behavior in response to new information or environments, is highly valued in Stoic practice. It allows us to remain open and adaptable in the face of life's constant changes. Cognitive flexibility can be cultivated through various strategies that challenge our existing beliefs and open us up to new perspectives and experiences. For instance, engaging with diverse viewpoints, whether through reading, conversation, or travel, can broaden our understanding and reduce the rigidity of our preconceptions. Another effective method is to practice scenario planning, where you envision different outcomes and strategize various responses. This not only prepares you for potential changes but also reduces anxiety about the unknown, as you've mentally equipped yourself to handle multiple possibilities.

Stoicism isn't just about personal resilience; it's deeply woven with virtues that guide our responses to every aspect of life, including change. The Stoic virtues of courage and wisdom are particularly pertinent when navigating through new phases. Courage in Stoicism involves more than bravery in the face of danger; it's about the moral courage to embrace change and the uncertainty it brings. It's about seeing the growth potential in new challenges and stepping forward with confidence, even when the path isn't obvious. Wisdom, on the other hand, helps us make decisions that are not based on fleeting emotions or superficial judgments but are rooted in a deep understanding of our values and the broader context of our lives. It enables us to discern which changes are beneficial and align with our long-term goals and which are distractions that lead us astray.

Practical steps are necessary for adapting to new circumstances effectively. Setting small, manageable goals is a powerful strategy during times of change. These goals can act as stepping stones that guide your path through unfamiliar territory, providing a sense of direction and accomplishment that bolsters your confidence and motivation. For example, if you're transitioning to a new career field, your initial goals might include networking with professionals in the industry or completing specific skill-building courses. Additionally, seeking support from Stoic communities or like-minded individuals can provide both practical advice and emotional encouragement. These communities, whether found in local meetups or online forums, offer a wealth of collective wisdom and experience that can be invaluable in navigating change. They remind us that we are not alone in our struggles and that shared human understanding is a reservoir from which we can all draw strength and insight.

By integrating these strategies into our lives, we not only equip ourselves to manage the inevitable changes that come our way but also transform our experience of these changes from something we have to endure into opportunities for personal growth and renewal. Through the mindful application of Stoic teachings—embracing change as a natural part of life, cultivating cognitive flexibility, leaning on core Stoic virtues, and taking practical steps for adaptation—we can navigate life's uncertainties not just with resilience but with a proactive enthusiasm that turns every change into a stepping stone towards a richer, more fulfilling life.

MAINTAINING A STOIC MINDSET DURING GLOBAL UNCERTAINTY

In a world where headlines often herald crises—from financial downturns to environmental disasters—the need to maintain a stoic mindset becomes not just helpful but essential. Stoicism teaches the art of living in the present moment, a skill that becomes particularly valuable during times of global uncertainty. By focusing our mental energy on the present, we shield ourselves from the paralyzing effects of worry about future events that are beyond our control. This practice is rooted in the understanding that anxiety often stems from hypothetical scenarios that may never materialize. Instead, Stoicism encourages us to engage directly with the here and now— where we can make actual, not imagined, differences.

Living in the present moment involves a conscious awareness of our current experiences and actions. It means acknowledging our feelings about global events but choosing not to be overwhelmed by uncertain future implications. For instance, consider the approach of a Stoic during an economic recession. Instead of being consumed by worry about potential job loss, the Stoic would focus on enhancing their current job performance and perhaps even taking steps to improve their skills, making themselves more valuable in the workplace. This focus on present actions allows for a sense of control and effectiveness that future-oriented worry never could.

Engagement in proactive behaviors is another fundamental aspect of maintaining a Stoic mindset in times of global uncertainty. Stoics are not passive observers of life; they are active participants who manage their actions within their sphere of influence. Staying informed about international events, preparing for reasonable outcomes, and contributing positively to one's community are all proactive behaviors endorsed by Stoicism. For example, in the face of an impending natural disaster, a Stoic would focus on preparing their home and helping neighbors secure their properties. By concentrating on these actionable steps, they maintain a sense of personal agency and community responsibility, which are crucial to Stoic ethics.

The concept of Stoic acceptance plays a pivotal role in how we respond to global uncertainties. This acceptance is not about resignation or passivity; instead, it's about acknowledging the reality of a situation without letting it dictate our inner state. Acceptance allows us to see the world as it is, not as we wish it to be, and this clarity of vision enables us to act more effectively. When we accept that certain aspects of global events are beyond our control, we can direct our energies towards more fruitful endeavors—those within our power to change. This Stoic acceptance can be particularly empowering in environmental activism, where the scale of global challenges can seem daunting. Activists who embrace Stoic principles focus their efforts on achievable projects and community education, thus making tangible impacts without becoming overwhelmed by the broader issues beyond their control.

Historical examples abound of Stoics who maintained their composure and integrity in the face of significant societal challenges. One poignant instance is Cato the Younger, a Roman statesman who often found himself at odds with Julius Caesar. Despite the upheaval and the personal risk of opposing Caesar, Cato remained steadfastly committed to his principles, embodying Stoic virtues such as courage and justice. His life, particularly his refusal to compromise his ethical standards despite extreme pressure, offers a powerful lesson in maintaining moral integrity during times of political turmoil. In a more contemporary context, consider the calm persistence of individuals who continued to advocate for social justice and human rights even when faced with social backlash or indifference. Their resilience in the face of adversity is a modern reflection of Stoic endurance and commitment to virtue.

These narratives not only inspire but also guide us in applying Stoic principles to our own lives, especially in times of global uncertainty. By focusing on the present, engaging in proactive behaviors, practicing acceptance, and drawing inspiration from those who have navigated crises with Stoic grace, we, too, can cultivate a mindset that turns challenges into opportunities for growth and affirmation of our deepest values. In doing so, we uphold the Stoic ideal of living a life of purpose and resilience, regardless of the external circumstances we face.

THE STOIC'S PATH TO RECOVERY AND REBUILDING AFTER SETBACKS

In the Stoic view, setbacks are not mere obstacles or defeats; they are catalysts for growth and self-discovery. This perspective is fundamental to understanding how Stoicism transforms our approach to life's inevitable downturns. Unlike the common perception that setbacks are purely negative, Stoicism invites us to see them as valuable opportunities to practice virtues such as resilience, moderation, and wisdom. These moments challenge us not only to endure but to expand our capacities and fortify our character.

The initial phase of dealing with any setback involves a constructive response. Rather than succumbing to frustration or despair, Stoicism teaches us to engage with these challenges actively and thoughtfully. This engagement is not about quick fixes but about a deep, sustained commitment to learning from every experience. For instance, if a project at work fails to yield the expected results, instead of viewing this as a failure, a Stoic approach would be to analyze the process critically—what were the strengths, and what could be improved? This mindset shifts the focus from what went wrong to what we can learn, setting the stage for more effective future endeavors.

Rebuilding one's life or work after a setback is significantly enriched by the application of Stoic principles. Resilience, a critical Stoic virtue, involves more than mere endurance; it encompasses the ability to recover gracefully and emerge stronger. This resilience can be cultivated through regular reflection on personal experiences, assessing not just outcomes but the thought processes and decisions that led to those outcomes. Moderation plays a crucial role as well, helping to maintain balance amid the highs and lows of recovery. It guards against extremes of overconfidence or despair, promoting a steady and sustainable path forward. Wisdom, the third pillar, guides the decision-making process, ensuring that each step taken is aligned with one's deeper values and long-term objectives.

A practical approach to rebuilding after setbacks involves a structured, step-by-step roadmap that emphasizes long-term growth and continuous adaptation of Stoic principles. This roadmap might start with setting clear, achievable goals that build on the lessons learned from the setback. Each goal should be specific and have a time limit, providing a clear path for progress and reassessment. Regular reflection is crucial—this could be a weekly review of what was accomplished, what challenges were encountered, and how they were addressed. This practice not only ensures adherence to Stoic principles but also fosters a habit of mindful engagement with one's progress and setbacks.

Adaptation is another critical component of this roadmap. The Stoic practice of remaining open to new information and experiences allows for the flexibility needed to adjust plans as circumstances evolve. This dynamic approach ensures that strategies remain relevant and responsive to real-world conditions, enhancing the effectiveness of the recovery process. Additionally, the pursuit of virtue, which is central to Stoic philosophy, should permeate every stage of this roadmap. Whether in setting goals, reflecting on progress, or adapting strategies, the commitment to practicing virtues such as honesty, courage, and humility should guide all actions and decisions.

This structured yet flexible approach not only aids in recovery but also transforms the experience of dealing with setbacks. It shifts the narrative from one of recovery to one of opportunity—where each setback becomes a chance to refine strategies, strengthen virtues, and deepen understanding. This transformation is not about returning to a previous state but about reaching new heights of personal and professional development.

In essence, the Stoic's path to recovery and rebuilding is a journey marked by continuous learning, ethical growth, and strategic adaptation. It is a process that not only restores but enhances, guided by a philosophy that sees every challenge as a doorway to greater wisdom and strength. As we wrap up this exploration of Stoicism in times of crisis, let us carry forward the lessons learned here—not only to navigate setbacks when they arise but to transform them into profound opportunities for growth and renewal. These strategies, rooted in ancient wisdom, provide us with the tools not just to survive but to thrive, crafting lives of resilience, purpose, and deep fulfillment.

As we conclude this chapter, we reflect on the transformative power of Stoic philosophy in times of crisis. From finding strength in loss to navigating unexpected changes, from maintaining composure in global uncertainty to recovering from setbacks, Stoicism offers a comprehensive framework for facing life's challenges with grace and wisdom. Let us move forward, equipped with these timeless strategies, ready to turn every obstacle into an opportunity for growth. As we transition into the next chapter, we will delve deeper into the practical applications of Stoicism in everyday life, exploring how these ancient principles can be seamlessly integrated into modern living to enhance our resilience, happiness, and overall well-being.

8

THE INTERSECTION OF STOICISM AND MODERN PSYCHOLOGY

As you navigate through the ebb and flow of everyday life, have you ever wondered how ancient philosophical insights could effectively intersect with modern psychological practices to enhance your mental wellness? This curiosity unveils a profound connection between Stoicism, a philosophy rooted in logic and personal ethics, and Cognitive Behavioral Therapy (CBT), a modern psychological approach that emphasizes the importance of thought patterns in influencing behavior and emotional health. This chapter explores the symphony between these two disciplines, revealing how they collectively offer a robust framework for managing thoughts, emotions, and behaviors in a way that promotes a healthier, more resilient mental state.

COGNITIVE BEHAVIORAL THERAPY AND STOICISM: A COMPARISON

Outline Similarities in Principles

Both Stoicism and Cognitive Behavioral Therapy (CBT) pivot on a central insight: our feelings and behaviors are significantly shaped by our thoughts. Stoicism, established in the bustling marketplaces of ancient Greece, teaches that it is not events themselves that disturb people but the views they take of them. Similarly, CBT, developed in the mid-20th century, operates on the understanding that changing dysfunctional thinking patterns can alter emotions and behaviors, leading to improved mental health and greater life satisfaction.

The commonalities between these two approaches are striking. Stoicism encourages individuals to discern between what is within their control—mainly their thoughts, motives, and actions—and what is not, which includes the actions and opinions of others and external events. CBT also empowers individuals to identify and modify distorted thinking, focusing on managing worry and anxiety by addressing how thoughts influence emotions and behaviors. Both philosophies believe in a proactive rather than reactive approach to mental challenges, emphasizing personal responsibility and the power of self-reflection.

Discuss the Concept of Cognitive Distortion

Cognitive distortions are irrational thought patterns that often lead to negative emotions and behaviors. These are central to CBT's diagnostic approach, where therapists help clients identify and challenge distorted thoughts. Stoicism, with its focus on perceptions, closely aligns with this concept. Stoics teach that by changing our perceptions, we can maintain serenity despite external circumstances. For instance, Epictetus famously said, "Men are disturbed not by things, but by the view which they take of them."

In practice, both Stoicism and CBT encourage individuals to engage in cognitive restructuring—a process of identifying and disputing irrational or dysfunctional thoughts. Stoicism uses techniques like the premeditation of evils, which involves contemplating potential adverse outcomes to diminish the distress they cause. At the same time, CBT employs similar strategies, such as worst-case scenario planning, helping individuals to assess and prepare realistically for potential challenges.

Provide Comparative Techniques

To illustrate the synergy between Stoicism and CBT, consider the technique of negative visualization, a Stoic exercise that involves contemplating the loss of things valued to reduce distress when such losses occur. Similarly, CBT's worst-case scenario technique encourages individuals to face their fears by visualizing the worst possible outcome and rationally planning responses, thereby reducing anxiety and increasing preparedness.

Both approaches also emphasize the importance of daily practice in developing mental resilience. For instance, Marcus Aurelius, a Stoic philosopher, kept a personal journal to reflect on and challenge his thoughts, a method akin to CBT's use of thought records where clients track dysfunctional thoughts and their emotional consequences to identify patterns and triggers.

Evaluate Effectiveness in Therapy

The integration of Stoic principles into CBT has been evidenced to enhance therapeutic outcomes, particularly in treating anxiety and depression. Studies indicate that individuals who employ Stoic practices such as focusing on the controllable, accepting the inevitable, and practicing mindfulness report lower levels of stress and higher life satisfaction. Clinical observations also suggest that incorporating Stoic exercises into CBT sessions helps clients manage emotional disturbances better, fostering a more balanced and proactive approach to mental health challenges.

The convergence of Stoicism and Cognitive Behavioral Therapy offers a compelling toolkit for anyone seeking to understand and improve their mental health. By grounding modern psychological practices in Stoic wisdom, individuals are equipped with a time-tested yet scientifically supported framework for navigating the complexities of the mind, ensuring a journey toward greater emotional resilience and psychological well-being. As we delve deeper into the practical applications of this synergy, you may discover not only the science of mental health but also the art of living well.

STOICISM AND MINDFULNESS: TECHNIQUES FOR THE PRESENT MOMENT

Mindfulness, in both psychological and Stoic contexts, revolves around the cultivation of a heightened state of awareness and presence in the current moment. Psychologically, mindfulness is viewed as the practice of being attentively present and consciously aware of our thoughts, emotions, and environment without judgment or distraction. In Stoicism, mindfulness aligns closely with the concept of Prosoche, which is the practice of attentive and vigilant self-awareness of one's thoughts and actions in accordance with reason. Both disciplines hold that mindfulness is not merely a passive state but an active pursuit of clarity aimed at enhancing rational thinking and emotional equanimity.

The practice of mindfulness in modern psychology often involves meditation techniques that encourage individuals to observe their thoughts and feelings without attachment, thereby gaining greater control over their responses. Stoicism offers a parallel through exercises like the 'view from above,' where one visualizes one's life from a broader perspective, fostering a sense of the temporal and spatial smallness of one's concerns. This Stoic practice not only encourages a wider perspective but also diminishes the emotional impact of present worries, aligning closely with the psychological practice of mindfulness in reducing stress and anxiety.

Another Stoic practice, voluntary discomfort, involves intentionally placing oneself in uncomfortable situations to build resilience and reduce the fear of adversity. This could include fasting or taking cold showers. Similarly, in modern psychological practices, mindfulness might be cultivated through exposure to less comfortable situations to decrease sensitivity to stressors and increase the ability to manage them effectively. Both practices teach that discomfort can be a path to growth, reinforcing the idea that challenges should not be feared but used as opportunities for strengthening character and competence.

The benefits of mindfulness from a Stoic perspective converge on the concept of apatheia, or freedom from distress. By practicing mindfulness, you train yourself to detach from misleading perceptions and irrational impulses that can lead to distress. This Stoic goal is achieved by maintaining a focus on rational judgment and internal tranquility, irrespective of external circumstances. Modern psychological approaches echo this benefit, as mindfulness has been shown to significantly decrease symptoms in conditions such as depression, anxiety, and PTSD by helping individuals reframe their thoughts and reduce overwhelming emotional reactions.

For practical daily integration, consider starting with a simple mindfulness routine each morning. Spend a few minutes in quiet reflection, perhaps following the Stoic meditation on the dichotomy of control, focusing on distinguishing between what you can change and what you cannot. Throughout the day, take brief "mindfulness breaks" to assess your current state of mind. Ask yourself questions like, "Are my responses aligned with my values? Am I focusing on the present or worrying about the past or future?" These check-ins can help recenter your thoughts and ensure you are living true to Stoic principles and psychological best practices for mental well-being.

Incorporating these mindfulness techniques into your routine not only enhances your ability to live in the present but also fortifies your resilience against the stresses of daily life. Whether you are facing a challenging situation at work or navigating complex personal relationships, mindfulness offers a toolset that empowers you to manage your thoughts and emotions with clarity and purpose. By fostering a habit of mindful living, guided by both Stoic wisdom and psychological practices, you cultivate a life characterized by increased rationality, emotional stability, and overall serenity.

THE PSYCHOLOGICAL BENEFITS OF STOIC ACCEPTANCE

Acceptance, a concept both respected and vital within the realms of psychology and Stoic philosophy, serves as a cornerstone in managing psychological distress. In the psychological context, acceptance is often associated with therapies like Acceptance and Commitment Therapy (ACT), which emphasizes accepting whatever is out of personal control while committing to actions that enrich life. In Stoicism, acceptance is deeply ingrained in the philosophy's teachings, focusing on acknowledging the limits of our power over external events and only internalizing what we can influence—our perceptions, actions, and will.

Both Stoicism and ACT advocate for a form of acceptance that is active rather than passive. It's not about resigning oneself to fate but rather about recognizing the futility in resisting the unchangeable, thus channeling one's energy more productively. This form of acceptance is not about giving up but is an empowering state of acknowledging reality as it is, which paradoxically enables more significant change in one's life. Stoic acceptance, for instance, teaches that we should not be upset by the events themselves but rather by our opinions about them. This is echoed in ACT, which suggests that suffering comes less from the experience itself and more from our entangled reactions to the experience.

Embracing Stoic acceptance can lead to decreased emotional responsiveness. For example, consider someone dealing with chronic pain. A Stoic approach would be to urge this individual not to focus on the unfairness of the pain or the limitations it imposes but instead on their ability to respond to the pain with dignity and courage. This shift in focus from the uncontrollable (the existence of pain) to the controllable (the response to pain) can lead to significant decreases in emotional disturbances like anger and depression, thereby fostering superior emotional equilibrium.

Moreover, Stoic acceptance enhances resilience by cultivating an attitude of equanimity towards life's ups and downs. It teaches that while we cannot control external events, we can control our perceptions and reactions, which in turn shape our reality. This view is crucial during significant life transitions, such as during the loss of a loved one. In such times, Stoic acceptance helps individuals navigate their grief by allowing them to experience their emotions without being overwhelmed by them. It encourages the bereaved to appreciate the time they had with the person and to accept the loss as part of the natural course of life, thus supporting a healthier grieving process.

One effective exercise to cultivate Stoic acceptance involves the practice of imagining life without a loved, cherished possession or even personal ability. This visualization not only prepares one for potential losses but also enhances appreciation for the present, fostering a mindset that is more resistant to disturbances when changes occur. This method, known as negative visualization, is not about pessimism; instead, it's about tempering the soul to face any of life's realities without despair.

Another strategy involves systematic exposure to personal fears or discomforts. For instance, if one fears public speaking, the Stoic practice would involve gradually exposing oneself to speaking in front of others, starting with small, supportive groups and slowly increasing the audience size. This practice not only reduces the fear over time but also empowers the individual, reinforcing their capacity to handle previously daunting situations.

In these ways, Stoic acceptance serves as a powerful tool in the psychological toolkit, offering strategies that lead to a life characterized not by avoidance of hardship but by graceful acceptance and proactive engagement with the world. Through these practices, you learn to hold a calm center, even as the storms of life rage around you, ensuring that when changes come, you are not uprooted.

RESILIENCE TRAINING: PSYCHOLOGICAL INSIGHTS FROM STOIC EXERCISES

Resilience, a term frequently spotlighted in both psychological circles and Stoic discussions, encapsulates more than just the ability to recover from setbacks; it involves a profound capacity to adapt and thrive regardless of difficulties. From a psychological perspective, resilience is often defined as the ability to bounce back from adversity, maintaining functional psychological and physical baseline levels. Stoicism, however, enriches this understanding by emphasizing not only the capacity to endure but also the ability to preserve virtue and steadfastness under pressure. This nuanced view suggests that resilience is not merely about returning to a former state but evolving through challenges in a way that aligns with one's ethical values.

Often, Stoic practices that foster resilience involve exercises that push the individual beyond their comfort zone, thus fortifying their mental and emotional defenses. One such practice is voluntary hardship, which includes intentionally engaging in challenging activities like fasting, sleeping on the floor, or avoiding comforts like air conditioning. These practices are not masochistic but are designed to strengthen one's fortitude against future hardships, much like a muscle grows stronger through exertion. Another key Stoic exercise is reflective contemplation, where one reviews one's day to evaluate one's responses to various challenges. This practice cultivates a mindful awareness of one's reactions and promotes a habit of learning from every situation.

These Stoic exercises share a striking resemblance with modern psychological resilience training programs. Such programs often incorporate elements such as exposure to controlled stressors, which help individuals develop coping strategies and reduce sensitivity to anxiety triggers. Similarly, reflective processing—akin to Stoic contemplation—urges individuals to learn from past experiences, thereby enhancing their ability to handle future stresses more effectively.

Various studies and observations support the effectiveness of integrating Stoic practices into resilience training. For instance, research within military training environments, where resilience is critical, has shown that soldiers exposed to pre-deployment training that includes Stoic principles, such as controlling focus under pressure and maintaining mental clarity in chaos, perform better in high-stress situations. Similarly, high-stress occupations such as emergency services have benefited from resilience training that incorporates Stoic exercises, helping professionals maintain calm and effective responses in crises.

In sports psychology, the incorporation of Stoic practices, like focusing only on controllable aspects of the game, has been linked to improved performance and mental endurance among athletes. These individuals learn to maintain focus during competitions, manage anxiety, and maintain a performance-enhancing mindset despite the high-pressure environment. This Stoic approach helps athletes not only during the event but in their overall mental preparedness and recovery from setbacks, whether they are injuries or losses.

Incorporating these Stoic resilience-building practices into your daily life can simply start, for instance, by choosing to practice voluntary hardship—skipping a meal or turning off your electronic devices for several hours one day a week. Reflect on this experience at the end of the day, noting any feelings of discomfort and your reactions to them. Over time, these small exercises can significantly enhance your resilience, preparing you for more significant life challenges and enabling a more stoic response to adversity.

By integrating Stoic exercises into modern resilience training, you tap into a wellspring of historical wisdom that complements contemporary psychological practices. This synergy not only enriches our understanding of resilience but also broadens the tools available for developing this crucial trait. Through these practices, you are not just equipped to handle the inevitable difficulties of life but also emerge from them more assertive, virtuous, and steadfast.

In this exploration of resilience from both Stoic and psychological viewpoints, we've uncovered how ancient practices can bolster modern mental fitness. As we transition from understanding individual resilience to exploring community resilience in the next chapter, remember that the principles of Stoicism extend beyond personal development. They also offer a blueprint for building stronger, more supportive communities that can withstand and thrive through collective challenges.

9

STOICISM AND THE PURSUIT OF HAPPINESS

In the midst of life's relentless pace, where the pursuit of 'happiness' often leads us down paths of fleeting pleasures and superficial achievements, how do we anchor our happiness in something more enduring and less vulnerable to life's inevitable fluctuations? Stoicism, a philosophical beacon from antiquity, offers a profound and lasting interpretation of happiness that challenges the conventional chase for ephemeral delights, guiding us instead towards a life of virtue and internal contentment.

DEFINING HAPPINESS IN STOIC TERMS

Happiness, or 'Eudaimonia' as we know it in Stoic philosophy, transcends the modern interpretation of fleeting emotional highs or the accumulation of material successes. Instead, it is conceived as the profound joy that arises from living a life aligned with virtue and rationality. This Stoic happiness is cultivated through deliberate ethical living and self-mastery, making it almost impervious to external circumstances and vicissitudes.

The distinction between Stoic happiness and hedonistic pleasure is pivotal. Hedonism, which advocates the pursuit of pleasure and the avoidance of pain, often results in happiness that relies upon external conditions—thus, it is inherently unstable and fleeting. Stoicism criticizes this dependence on external sources for happiness, proposing instead that true contentment comes from within, from living a life according to nature's rational order and one's rational nature.

A unique aspect of Stoic philosophy is the concept of 'preferred indifferents.' These are external things—such as wealth, health, and reputation—that, while not necessary for happiness, can be pursued and enjoyed if one acquires them in a manner that does not compromise one's virtue. The Stoics teach that while these 'indifferents' may facilitate a comfortable life, they should never be the source of our happiness, nor should their loss or absence be a source of great distress. This perspective inspires a balanced approach to life's external offerings, appreciating and utilizing them without becoming overly attached or dependent.

The lives of notable Stoics such as Seneca and Epictetus exemplify this approach to happiness. Seneca, a wealthy man by any standard, used his resources to foster his philosophical pursuits yet remained detached from the wealth itself, often writing about the virtues of simplicity and the dangers of affluence. Epictetus, born into slavery, found his freedom not through external emancipation—which he eventually did receive—but through his determined focus on internal growth and understanding. Both figures demonstrated that Stoic happiness is achieved not through the possession of material goods or favorable circumstances but through the cultivation of virtue, wisdom, and inner resilience.

VISUAL ELEMENT: STOIC TREE OF VIRTUE AND HAPPINESS

The Stoic Tree of Virtue and Happiness (Infographic)

- Roots: Core Stoic Virtues (Wisdom, Courage, Justice, Temperance)
- Trunk: Stoic Practices (Reflection, Discipline, Mindfulness)
- Branches: Preferred Indifferents (Wealth, Health, Success)
- Leaves: Eudaimonia (Joy and Contentment derived from Virtuous Living)

This visual metaphor illustrates how the robust 'roots' of Stoic virtues support the enduring 'trunk' of daily Stoic practices, which in turn bear the 'leaves' of true happiness, irrespective of the 'branches' of external circumstances that may sway in the winds of fortune.

Through Stoicism, we reexamine our understanding of happiness, prompting a shift from seeking external validation or fleeting pleasures to fostering an inner citadel of virtue and wisdom. As we align our lives with these Stoic principles, we discover that true happiness is not something that is chased and caught; it is cultivated and lived, a byproduct of a life well-lived in accordance with reason and virtue. This Stoic happiness, deeply rooted and nourished by ethical living, offers not only personal peace but also enriches the world around us, making it a profound goal worthy of pursuit.

DAILY STOIC PRACTICES TO ENHANCE LIFE SATISFACTION

In the pursuit of a life marked not just by success but by deep fulfillment and calm, Stoicism offers not just a philosophy but a daily practice. Integrating Stoic exercises into your daily routine isn't just about adhering to an ancient philosophy—it's about creating a life that's more reflective, responsive, and rich in contentment. For those looking to infuse their day-to-day lives with the wisdom of Stoicism, several practices can be seamlessly incorporated into even the busiest schedules.

Morning meditations on gratitude are a cornerstone of daily Stoic practice. This exercise involves taking a few quiet moments each morning to reflect on what you are thankful for. It could range from appreciating the simple comfort of a home to acknowledging a loved one's support or even valuing the challenges that provide opportunities for growth. This practice sets an attitude of positivity and appreciation for the day ahead, anchoring you in a mindset that values what you have rather than what you lack. The Stoic emphasis on gratitude is profound because it shifts focus from external desires to internal wealth, fostering a sense of abundance that is not contingent on material possessions or status.

Evening reviews of actions are equally crucial. This practice involves taking time at the end of the day to reflect on your actions and decisions. Did they align with your Stoic values? How did you respond to stress or an unexpected challenge? Did you act out of impulse or from a place of reasoned decision-making? This introspection not only aids in personal growth by highlighting areas of improvement but also reinforces your commitment to living stoically. Over time, this routine nurtures a reflective mind that naturally leans towards making more considered and honorable choices.

Mindfulness during routine tasks is another practical Stoic exercise. It involves being fully present and engaged in the current activity without judgment or distraction. Whether you're washing dishes, driving, or typing an email, mindfulness turns these ordinary tasks into moments of meditation and presence. This practice deepens your connection to the present moment—a key Stoic aim—helping you cultivate a life where peace isn't something you seek from external sources but instead is something you generate from within.

Integrating Stoicism into Modern Life

Modern life, with its rapid pace and constant connectivity, can often feel at odds with the thoughtful, deliberate practice of Stoicism. However, there are numerous ways to weave Stoic exercises into the fabric of contemporary living. For instance, use your breaks at work to practice brief reflections or mindfulness exercises. Just a few minutes of focusing on your breath or contemplating a Stoic principle can reset your mind and reduce stress. Your commute can be transformed into an educational session by listening to audiobooks or podcasts on Stoicism, turning traffic jams into opportunities for learning and reflection.

Another tip is to set reminders on your phone or computer for Stoic reflections. These can be simple prompts, like "What are you grateful for?" or "What is within your control?" popping up throughout your day to realign your focus with Stoic ideals. This method ensures that Stoicism isn't just something you read about or think about in abstract terms—it becomes a lived experience integrated into the workings of daily life.

Success Stories

The transformative impact of these Stoic practices is not just theoretical. Many individuals have reported significant enhancements in their life satisfaction after integrating Stoicism into their daily routines. Take, for instance, a corporate lawyer who started practicing morning gratitude meditations. She reported a noticeable decrease in her usual stress levels and an increase in her overall job satisfaction. She attributed these changes to her new-found ability to appreciate her achievements and the positive aspects of her challenging job. Another example is a stay-at-home parent who found that practicing mindfulness during routine tasks helped manage the day-to-day stresses of parenting, making him more present and patient.

These testimonies underscore a crucial truth about Stoicism: it is profoundly practical. Its practices are designed not just for the quiet of meditation rooms or the isolation of retreats but for the rough and tumble of everyday life. They provide tools to transform not just how you think but how you live, bringing a depth of satisfaction that endures beyond changing circumstances and fleeting pleasures. As you continue to explore and integrate these practices into your daily life, you may find that Stoicism offers not just a philosophy or a set of practices but a roadmap to a highly fulfilling way of living.

BALANCING AMBITION AND CONTENTMENT: A STOIC PERSPECTIVE

Ambition and contentment might seem like opposing forces, yet Stoicism presents a unique framework where both can coexist harmoniously, enriching one's life rather than pulling it apart. The Stoic approach to ambition does not dismiss it but instead refines its direction and purpose. It encourages the pursuit of excellence and meaningful goals, but crucially, these goals are to be pursued in alignment with virtuous living and ethical principles. This perspective ensures that ambition does not overrun ethical considerations or personal integrity, keeping us grounded in what truly enriches our lives.

In the realm of Stoicism, ambition is viewed as a positive force when it drives us to improve ourselves and contribute to the world in meaningful ways. However, this improvement and contribution must always adhere to Stoic virtues such as wisdom, justice, courage, and moderation. For instance, ambition that leads to cutthroat competition or unethical behaviors for personal gain is unambiguously against Stoic values. Instead, Stoics advocate for ambitions that elevate not only the individual but also those around them, fostering a collective well-being.

The balance between ambition and contentment is also maintained by embracing contentment with the present. While it's natural to strive for future goals, finding joy in the current moment and appreciating what we already have is equally important. This does not mean complacency or abandoning future aspirations but recognizing and valuing the richness of the present. Such contentment is cultivated through gratitude, mindfulness, and acceptance—practices that anchor us amidst the often tumultuous pursuit of our goals. By fostering contentment with the present, we protect ourselves from the disenchantment that can come if ambitions are delayed or derailed. It helps maintain an internal balance, ensuring that our well-being does not become dependent on external achievements.

Reflective goal-setting is a practical Stoic tool that bridges ambition with virtue. This involves setting goals that are not only ambitious but reflective of Stoic virtues, ensuring that our pursuits contribute positively to our character and overall happiness. When setting goals, ask yourself: Are these goals fostering my growth in virtue? Are they benefiting others as much as they benefit me? This reflective practice turns goal-setting into a disciplined exercise of self-awareness and ethical scrutiny, aligning our ambitions with our deepest values and ensuring that our pursuits are not just about reaching a destination but about enriching the journey there with integrity and purpose.

The lives of both historical and contemporary figures who have successfully balanced ambition with contentment offer inspiring illustrations of this Stoic ideal in action. Consider the story of Cato the Younger, a figure renowned in Stoic tradition for his unwavering integrity. Cato's political ambitions were driven by a deep commitment to the Roman Republic's ideals, advocating for justice and the rule of law despite the personal risks these stances entailed. His life demonstrates how ambition, when guided by staunch ethical principles, can pursue noble ends, even in the face of personal loss or failure.

In contemporary times, we see similar embodiments of Stoic balance in individuals like Malala Yousafzai, whose ambition for educational equality deeply intertwines with her commitment to peace and justice. Despite immense challenges and threats, her goals remain steadfastly aligned with her virtues, inspiring millions worldwide. Her journey underscores the fact that true ambition, informed by Stoic principles, looks beyond personal achievement to the broader impact of one's actions on the community and the world.

This Stoic approach to balancing ambition with contentment invites us to rethink our pursuits and the values that underpin them. It inspires us to aim high but with a foundation firmly rooted in virtue and ethical living. As you reflect on your ambitions and the contentment you derive from your present, consider how you can weave them together through Stoic wisdom, not only to achieve external success but to cultivate a life of profound internal richness and peace.

THE ROLE OF COMMUNITY AND RELATIONSHIPS IN STOIC HAPPINESS

In the tapestry of Stoic philosophy, the threads of community and relationships are not merely decorative but structurally vital. Stoicism, often misconstrued as a doctrine of personal endurance and detached rationality, places profound importance on the fabric of community and the quality of our relationships. This emphasis is rooted in the belief that virtues like justice and charity are not practiced in isolation but portray our interactions with others. The Stoic concept of internationalism extends this idea on a global scale, advocating for a worldview where every human interaction is an opportunity to practice these virtues, treating all individuals with fairness and kindness regardless of their cultural or geographical distinctions.

This Stoic principle of internationalism is not just an ideal but a practical approach to living. It encourages viewing oneself as a citizen of the world, which fosters a sense of responsibility towards fellow humans regardless of one's immediate social or cultural circles. This broadened perspective helps to cultivate a sense of connectedness and empathy, reducing prejudices and promoting a more inclusive approach to social interactions. By embracing this global citizenship, you not only expand your own social and emotional horizons but also contribute to a more harmonious and understanding world.

Engaging in healthy relationships and community activities offers fertile ground for practicing Stoic virtues. Each interaction, whether it's volunteering at a local shelter, participating in a community clean-up, or simply lending an empathetic ear to a friend, serves as a practical application of Stoic teachings. These activities provide real-life scenarios where you can cultivate virtues like charity, justice, and temperance. For instance, volunteering allows for the practice of charity and empathy, pushing you to consider the well-being of others and offering your skills and time for their benefit. Similarly, resolving conflicts within your community or family with fairness and patience allows you to practice justice and temperance, balancing your own emotions and judgments with the needs and views of others.

Stoicism teaches that you will not achieve true happiness—Eudaimonia—through solitary pursuit but through contributions to the welfare of others, which in turn enriches our own lives. This reciprocal enhancement of contentment is evident in relationships that rely on principles of mutual respect, understanding, and support. Healthy relationships foster a supportive environment where individuals feel valued and connected, which significantly contributes to overall life satisfaction and resilience. These relationships become the channels through which Stoic virtues are not only practiced but also received, creating a cycle of positive interactions and personal growth.

Guidelines for Fostering Community Connections

Building and maintaining relationships that reflect Stoic principles is both a rewarding and challenging endeavor. Here are some practical guidelines to foster such connections:

- Volunteer Regularly: Engage in community service or volunteer work that aligns with your values. This not only benefits others but also enriches your own life, providing perspective and deepening your sense of gratitude and purpose.
- Participate in Discussion Groups: Whether it's a book club, a philosophy discussion group, or a community meeting, participation in these groups offers opportunities to exchange ideas, challenge your perceptions, and gain insights from diverse perspectives.
- Cultivate Open and Honest Communication: In your relationships, strive for transparency and honesty. This fosters trust and understanding, which are the essential components of any strong relationship.
- Practice Active Listening: Show genuine interest in others' thoughts and feelings. Active listening involves more than

just hearing the words; it's about understanding the underlying emotions and intentions, which can significantly deepen interpersonal bonds.

By integrating these practices into your daily life, you actively contribute to a community where Stoic virtues are not just idealized but lived. Each act of kindness, each moment of honest interaction, and each decision made with fairness and consideration reverberates, influencing not only your happiness but also the well-being of the community at large.

As this chapter on the role of community and relationships in Stoic happiness concludes, we see how deeply interwoven our individual well-being is with the health of our relationships and communities. Stoicism, far from promoting solitary introspection, inspires active participation in the world—engaging with, learning from, and contributing to the community around us. This is not a divergence from the pursuit of personal happiness but a vital part of it, enriching our lives with depth, purpose, and joy.

In the next chapter, we will explore how the principles of Stoicism can be applied to modern ethical dilemmas, providing a Stoic lens through which to view and address some of the most pressing issues facing our world today.

ADVANCED STOIC WISDOM

As you delve deeper into the rich tapestry of Stoicism, you encounter intriguing contradictions that challenge the surface-level understanding of this philosophical stronghold. Imagine standing at a crossroads where paths marked by seemingly opposing signs—'Freedom in Chains' and 'Wealth in Want'—intersect. Here lies the fascinating dominion of Stoic paradoxes, profound statements that at first glance appear contradictory yet reveal deeper truths upon closer examination. These paradoxes are not mere wordplay but are designed to provoke thought, challenge conventional wisdom, and deepen your understanding of Stoic philosophy.

NAVIGATING THE STOIC PARADOXES

Stoicism presents several paradoxes that may initially puzzle the uninitiated. Consider the statement, "the sage is free while in chains," or "true wealth consists in having few wants." To the modern mind, accustomed to equating freedom with physical liberty and wealth with material abundance, these assertions might seem contradictory, even irrational. However, these paradoxes serve a critical function in Stoic philosophy, pushing you to reconsider your assumptions about what it means to be free, wealthy, or happy.

The first paradox, "the sage is free while in chains," challenges the conventional notion of freedom. In Stoicism, true freedom is not about external circumstances but about one's internal state. A sage, or a wise person fully practicing Stoic principles, remains free even in physical bondage because their peace and happiness are not reliant on external conditions but are rooted in their virtuous character and rational mind. This idea encourages you to reflect on the nature of your own freedoms. Are they dependent on external validations and conditions, or are they grounded in something more profound and more enduring within you?

Similarly, the paradox "wealth consists in having few wants" turns the typical understanding of wealth on its head. Stoicism teaches that true wealth comes not from an abundance of possessions but from a paucity of desires. By limiting your desires to what is necessary and within your control, you achieve a kind of wealth that is impervious to external fluctuations. This paradox prompts you to evaluate your desires and consumption habits. Are they contributing to genuine happiness and fulfillment, or are they merely chaining you to endless cycles of wanting and acquiring?

Philosophical Interpretations

Various Stoic thinkers have offered insights into these paradoxes. Epictetus, for instance, emphasized the liberating power of self-control and rationality, suggesting that one can be 'free' in any circumstance if one maintains control over one's thoughts and desires. Seneca, on the other hand, broadly explored the concept of wealth, arguing that true riches entail wisdom, virtue, and peace of mind—qualities that are not diminished by external poverty.

These interpretations underline a common theme in Stoic thought: the redefinition of conventional values to align with virtue and rationality. By understanding these philosophical elucidations, you gain not only a more profound comprehension of Stoic paradoxes but also practical guidance on embodying Stoic principles in your daily life.

Encouraging Reflective Engagement

To engage more with these paradoxes, consider incorporating them into your reflective practices. Journaling, for example, can be an excellent way to explore these concepts. Dedicate a section of your journal to pondering these paradoxes. Write about times when you felt 'free' despite external constraints, or reflect on what 'wealth' truly means to you. How do these reflections change your perspective on freedom and wealth?

Additionally, joining or forming discussion groups can provide diverse perspectives on these paradoxes, enriching your understanding and application of Stoic principles. These conversations can challenge your viewpoints, deepen your insights, and help you see practical ways to integrate Stoic wisdom into your life.

Navigating the paradoxes of Stoicism not only enhances your understanding of this philosophical tradition but also enriches your personal and spiritual growth. By challenging orthodox definitions of freedom, wealth, and happiness, Stoicism invites you on a transformative path where wisdom and virtue illuminate the journey, offering a richer, deeper sense of fulfillment that transcends the superficial and fleeting pleasures of the material world.

ADVANCED TECHNIQUES IN STOIC MEDITATION AND REFLECTION

As you progress in your Stoic practice, you may find yourself seeking more advanced and nuanced ways to engage with this ancient philosophy. Progressive techniques in Stoic meditation and reflection offer profound avenues to enhance your sense of connectedness to the world and deepen your understanding of yourself. One such practice is the contemplation of the cosmos, a meditation that extends your perspective beyond the proximity of daily concerns and fosters a profound sense of humility and belonging to a larger order.

Contemplation of the cosmos involves visualizing the vastness of the universe and your tiny, albeit significant, place within it. This practice not only puts the scale of human affairs into perspective but also aligns with the Stoic principle that everything is interconnected. By recognizing your part in the grand tapestry of existence, you cultivate a sense of gratitude and responsibility towards it. Such meditations are not just exercises in humility; they are reminders of our duty to live virtuously, as our actions contribute to the harmony or discord of the universe. To practice this, you might begin by visualizing the Earth from space, seeing it as a single point of light among many, and gradually expanding your view to include the stars and galaxies. Try to reflect on the interconnectedness of all things and the small yet significant role you play in this vast cosmos.

Another advanced technique involves the use of visualization to solidify Stoic principles in your character. Imagining yourself as the ideal Stoic sage can be a powerful exercise in embodying the virtues you aspire to. Picture how a sage would handle the situations you face: their calmness, their rationality, their kindness. Then, visualize yourself acting in the same way. This practice not only provides a clear model to strive towards but also helps bridge the gap between theoretical understanding and practical application. Similarly, envisaging oneself facing and overcoming fears can reinforce courage and resilience. By mentally rehearsing your successful navigation of dreaded scenarios, you build confidence and psychologically prepare yourself to face the challenges ahead.

Deep reflection techniques also play a crucial role in advanced Stoic practice. Unlike daily reflections, which might focus on immediate reactions and events, deeper reflective practices involve a more thorough analysis of your progress in virtue. The philosophical diary is an essential tool in this regard. Instead of simple entries, this diary involves detailed examinations of your thoughts, actions, and their alignment with Stoic principles over more extended periods—weekly or monthly. This could include reflections on how well you maintained equanimity in stressful situations, how effectively you practiced justice in your interactions, or how you can better cultivate temperance in your desires and actions.

Connecting these practices to Stoic theories on psychology and ethics reveals their grounding in traditional thought while illustrating their evolution to address modern needs. Stoicism teaches that the development of virtue is the path to true happiness. Advanced meditation and reflection practices will deepen your engagement with these virtues and foster a transformation that is both profound and practical. By regularly engaging in these practices, you not only gain deeper insights into Stoic philosophy but also boost your ability to apply its teachings in everyday life, leading to a more thoughtful, balanced, and fulfilling existence.

THE STOIC RESPONSE TO MODERN ETHICAL DILEMMAS

In today's fast-evolving society, we grapple with ethical dilemmas that are complex and multifaceted, ranging from bioethical questions about genetic modifications to concerns about environmental sustainability and the moral intricacies of digital privacy. Stoicism, with its rich tradition of ethical reasoning, offers a robust framework for navigating these contemporary issues. By applying Stoic virtues—wisdom, justice, courage, and temperance—to modern dilemmas, you will find clarity and direction even in situations where the moral route seems obscured by competing interests and technological complexities.

Framing Bioethics Through Stoic Virtues

Consider the realm of bioethics, where advancements in genetic engineering and biotechnology present scenarios that our ancestors could scarcely have imagined. Stoicism teaches us to approach such challenges with wisdom and justice, balancing the potential benefits of scientific advancements with the ethical need to respect human dignity and the natural world. For instance, when considering the use of CRISPR technology for gene editing, Stoic wisdom could guide you in weighing the potential to eradicate hereditary diseases against the ethical implications of altering human genetics. The virtue of justice would demand an impartial consideration regarding who gets access to such technologies and the potential long-term impacts on society. In discussions or decision-making forums, advocating for policies that reflect not only scientific capabilities but also ethical responsibility embodies the Stoic commitment to virtue in the face of progress.

Environmental Ethics and Stoic Cosmopolitanism

Environmental concerns offer another area where Stoicism's principles are urgently needed. The Stoic view of cosmopolitanism —that all humans are citizens of the world—can be extended to include our stewardship of the planet. Applying Stoic justice involves advocating for actions that not only benefit individual communities but also contribute to global ecological balance. This could mean supporting sustainable practices that protect the environment and future generations, promoting a broader sense of responsibility and interconnectedness. Stoic courage comes into play when taking a stand against environmentally harmful practices, despite opposition from powerful interests or the apathy of convenience. Here, the Stoic is called to act with moral courage, championing the cause of environmental justice even when it is unpopular or economically challenging.

Navigating Digital Privacy with Stoic Principles

Digital privacy issues also call for a Stoic response. The rapid growth of digital technologies, while offering unprecedented connectivity and access to information, also raises significant concerns about privacy and the ethical use of data. Stoic wisdom guides you to discern the appropriate use of technology, balancing the benefits of digital innovation with the need to protect individual rights and freedoms. Temperance, or the virtue of moderation, plays a critical role in managing one's digital footprint, advocating for a balanced approach to technology that avoids the extremes of data exploitation or techno-phobia. By promoting policies and practices that safeguard personal information while supporting beneficial innovations, you embody Stoic virtues in addressing one of the most pressing moral dilemmas of our time.

Encouraging Active Ethical Practice

To actively engage with these dilemmas, Stoicism encourages not only reflection but also practical action. Consider implementing regular ethical audits in your professional and personal life, where you assess how well your actions align with your moral values. Such practices not only foster personal growth but also have a ripple effect, influencing others in your community and beyond. Engaging in community discussions or online forums about these issues can further your understanding and impact, allowing you to contribute Stoically to broader societal debates.

Stoicism, with its emphasis on virtue and rational discussion, provides a powerful lens through which to view and respond to modern ethical dilemmas. Whether navigating the complexities of bioethics, advocating for environmental justice, or managing digital privacy, the principles of Stoicism offer guidance that is both practical and profound, driving you to act not out of self-interest but in service of the greater good. By applying these timeless principles to contemporary issues, you continue the Stoic tradition of ethical engagement, promoting a more just, thoughtful, and virtuous society.

LONG-TERM STOICISM: SUSTAINING PRACTICE OVER A LIFETIME

Maintaining a Stoic practice throughout a lifetime presents its own unique set of challenges, which can vary significantly from one stage of life to another. One common issue you might encounter is a sense of doubt—doubt about the effectiveness of Stoicism in addressing new or evolving life circumstances or doubt stemming from the often foreseeable routine and complacency that can diminish the vibrancy of any long-practiced philosophy. Additionally, external pressures such as changes in personal relationships, career transitions, or significant global events can test the resilience of your Stoic practices. Furthermore, as you age and move through different phases of life, the significance and application of Stoic principles may seem to shift, requiring a flexible and adaptive approach to maintain their effectiveness.

To navigate these challenges and sustain your commitment to Stoicism, it is crucial to rejuvenate your practice regularly. One effective strategy is to delve back into the foundational texts of Stoicism. Re-reading the works of Marcus Aurelius, Seneca, and Epictetus can rekindle your enthusiasm and offer new insights that resonate with your current circumstances. Each reading at different stages of life can bring new meaning and perspective, deepening your understanding and appreciation of Stoic teachings.

Engaging with Stoic communities is another vital strategy. Whether it's participating in online forums, attending workshops, or joining local groups, connecting with others who are also walking the Stoic path can provide both inspiration and practical support. These communities offer a platform for sharing experiences and strategies, strengthening your practice through shared wisdom and encouragement. Additionally, assuming a teaching role within these communities can further solidify your understanding and commitment. Teaching others not only helps you clarify your own beliefs and practices but also provides a sense of purpose and fulfillment that comes from contributing to others' growth.

The practice of Stoicism is not static; it evolves as you grow and as your life circumstances change. What was impactful in your youth may take on a different significance in later years. Recognizing and embracing this dynamic nature of Stoic practice is the key to maintaining its importance and usefulness. For instance, while the focus in earlier years might be on harnessing ambition and managing external challenges, later years might shift towards reflecting on one's legacy and cultivating tranquility. Adapting your practice to these changing priorities and circumstances ensures that Stoicism continues to provide guidance and comfort throughout your life.

The lifelong benefits of sustained Stoic practice are profound. Stories from long-term practitioners often highlight a deep-seated sense of peace, resilience, and fulfillment that pervades their lives. They speak of a robust composure that buffers them against the vagaries of life and a clarity of purpose that guides their choices and interactions. These stories not only serve as a testament to the enduring power of Stoicism but also as a beacon to newer practitioners, illustrating the profound impact that Stoicism can have when integrated into one's life over the long term.

In this chapter, we have explored the challenges of maintaining a Stoic practice throughout life and discussed strategies to rejuvenate and adapt this practice to ensure its ongoing effectiveness and relevance. We've also considered how the evolving nature of Stoic practice reflects the changing stages and circumstances of life, providing a flexible framework that supports a lifetime of growth and fulfillment. As we transition to the next chapter, we will delve deeper into specific Stoic practices that can help you navigate the complexities of modern life, offering tools and strategies that are both practical and transformative. This exploration will not only supplement your understanding of Stoic philosophy but also improve your ability to apply its principles in a way that enriches your everyday life.

11

CREATING A STOIC MINDSET

I n the tapestry of life, each thread—every decision, action, and thought—intertwines to form the intricate pattern of our existence. But how often do we pause to consider the quality of these threads or the mindfulness with which we weave them? Stoicism, a philosophy designed for living well, provides the basis upon which we can create a life of purpose, resilience, and tranquility. This chapter invites you to integrate Stoic mindfulness into your daily routine, transforming ordinary moments into opportunities for growth and reflection.

CULTIVATING STOIC MINDFULNESS THROUGHOUT THE DAY

Mindfulness, in the Stoic sense, is not merely an act of meditation but a continuous thread that runs through the fabric of our daily lives. It involves a conscious focus on the present moment, an acceptance of what it brings, and a commitment to embody Stoic virtues in every action. Integrating Stoic mindfulness into your daily activities begins with the easiest yet most profound technique: conscious breathing.

Consider this: each breath you take is a new beginning, a moment ripe with potential for clarity and calm. By focusing on your breath, you anchor yourself in the present, steering your mind away from the clutter of past regrets and future anxieties. This practice can be employed anytime, anywhere—from the quiet of your morning routine to the chaos of a busy workday. Picture yourself in a stressful meeting; as tensions rise, you turn your focus inward to your breath, each inhalation and exhalation a reminder of your ability to maintain serenity and think clearly, embodying the Stoic ideal of tranquility amidst turmoil.

Building on this foundation of conscious breathing, you can further enrich your Stoic practice by integrating focused attention into your everyday tasks. Whether you are typing an email, cooking a meal, or engaging in conversation, fully immerse yourself in the activity. This means observing each sensation and action with inquisitiveness and detachment, recognizing that these are tasks within your control, and your mindful engagement with them can transform mundane routines into acts of philosophical practice.

To maintain this mindful state throughout the day, consider setting up intermittent reminders for Stoic reflections. These can be simple alerts on your phone or sticky notes placed in your workspace, each prompting you to pause and reflect on a Stoic virtue or the dichotomy of control. For instance, a reminder might prompt you to reflect on the virtue of temperance before a lunch meeting, encouraging you to make choices that align with your values rather than impulses.

Encouraging the Practice of 'Stoic Pauses'

Another powerful technique to enhance your daily Stoicism is the practice of 'Stoic pauses.' These are deliberate, short breaks taken at regular intervals—perhaps hourly or between major tasks—during which you withdraw from outward activities to realign with your Stoic principles. During a Stoic pause, you might step away from your desk to reflect on the events of the past hour, assessing your responses and adjustments needed to align more closely with Stoic virtues. This practice is valuable in high-pressure environments where reactive decisions can lead to regrettable outcomes. By routinely readjusting your approach, you ensure that your actions continue to be thoughtful and consistent with Stoic wisdom.

The benefits of cultivating continuous Stoic mindfulness are manifold. Emotionally, it helps regulate your responses, reducing the intensity of adverse reactions to stress or provocation. Practically, it increases your resilience to daily stressors as you become better equipped to handle challenges with a calm and focused mind. In decision-making, mindfulness enhances your clarity, allowing you to make choices that are not only reactive to immediate circumstances but also reflective of long-term goals and values. Ultimately, the continuous practice of Stoic mindfulness enriches your life satisfaction, as it nurtures a deeper engagement with the present and a more harmonious alignment with your philosophical ideals.

Incorporating these Stoic practices into your daily life does not require monumental changes but relatively small, consistent adjustments to your focus and actions. As you weave mindfulness into the fabric of your daily activities, you transform ordinary moments into profound opportunities for growth, embodying the Stoic ideals of wisdom, courage, justice, and temperance in all that you do.

THE IMPORTANCE OF ROUTINE AND DISCIPLINE IN STOICISM

In the realm of Stoicism, discipline is not merely a practice but the bedrock upon which the structure of a Stoic life is built. It is the discipline that enables the consistent application of Stoic principles, crafting a life marked by greater self-control, virtue, and, ultimately, peace. Stoicism teaches us that without discipline, our efforts to live a virtuous life are scattered and sporadic, susceptible to the caprices of circumstance and emotion. With discipline, however, we forge a steady path through life's ups and downs, our actions and thoughts deeply rooted in Stoic wisdom.

Imagine starting each day not as a series of random events but as a well-structured narrative, each chapter flowing seamlessly into the next, guided by the principles of wisdom, courage, justice, and temperance. This is the power of a Stoic routine. Such a routine might begin with the early morning hours dedicated to meditation, perhaps focusing on the day ahead and the virtues you wish to embody. This practice sets the tone for the day, grounding you in a state of mindfulness and purpose. Following meditation, a period of reflection on Stoic texts can provide philosophical guidance, connecting you with the timeless wisdom of Stoic sages like Marcus Aurelius or Seneca. These readings act not only as intellectual exercises but as spiritual sustenance, nourishing your inner life and preparing you for the day's challenges.

As the day unfolds, structured time for reflecting on your actions and their alignment with Stoic principles can help reinforce your commitment to living virtuously. This could be a midday review, a pause to assess the morning's events or an evening reflection, a quiet time to contemplate the day's successes and areas for improvement. Such practices ensure that your actions remain in harmony with your values, fostering a sense of integrity and consistency in your life. Additionally, scheduling regular periods to review and realign your actions with your goals and principles helps mitigate the impact of distractions and procrastination, common obstacles that can derail even the most dedicated practitioners.

ADDRESSING THE CHALLENGES OF MAINTAINING DISCIPLINE

Maintaining such a disciplined routine, however, is not without its challenges. The modern world, with its myriad distractions—from the incessant pings of smartphones to the constant demands of work and family life—can make sustained Stoic practice seem like a Herculean task. Procrastination, too, often creeps in, tempting us to defer our Stoic duties in favor of instantaneous pleasures or apparently urgent tasks. Yet, it is precisely in overcoming these challenges that the true value of Stoic discipline is revealed.

Stoic strategies to combat these distractions are both practical and philosophical. One effective method is the setting of distinct, manageable goals for each Stoic practice, whether it be meditation, reading, or reflection. By breaking down each practice into small, achievable steps, the overwhelming nature of sustaining discipline becomes more manageable, and the satisfaction of completing each step provides ongoing motivation. Furthermore, the Stoic practice of premeditatio malorum, or the premeditation of evils, can be adapted to anticipate potential distractions or reasons for procrastination. By foreseeing these challenges and planning your responses, you fortify your routine against the unforeseen, ensuring that your Stoic practices remain intact.

CASE STUDIES OF SUCCESSFUL STOIC ROUTINES

The effectiveness of these strategies is not merely theoretical but is evidenced by numerous individuals who have successfully integrated Stoic routines into their lives, reaping significant benefits. Consider the case of a high-level executive who, despite the hectic pace of corporate life, has maintained a morning routine of Stoic reflection and meditation for over a decade. This practice has not only enhanced his decision-making skills and resilience in the face of corporate challenges but has also improved his relationships with colleagues and family, imbuing his interactions with patience and understanding.

Another inspiring example is a teacher who incorporates Stoic principles into her daily interactions with students. By reflecting on Stoic virtues each morning and reviewing her day each evening, she has created a classroom environment that not only fosters academic excellence but also cultivates character and virtue among her students. Her disciplined adherence to Stoic practices has transformed her classroom into a space of growth and inquiry, benefiting both herself and her students.

These case studies highlight the transformative potential of a disciplined Stoic routine. By steadfastly applying Stoic principles through a structured daily schedule, individuals from all walks of life can achieve a more profound sense of fulfillment, resilience, and peace.

USING STOIC WISDOM TO SHAPE YOUR LIFE PHILOSOPHY

In the mosaic of your life, each piece—whether it's a fleeting moment or a significant event—holds the potential to contribute to the all-encompassing picture of who you are and what you stand for.

Stoicism, with its rich heritage and profound insights, offers ageless principles that can help you mold these pieces into a coherent and meaningful whole. Integrating Stoic principles into your core beliefs isn't just about adopting a new way of thinking; it's about transforming your entire approach to life, ensuring that every decision and action resonates with philosophical harmony.

Imagine your core beliefs as the foundation of a building. Just as a strong foundation supports and stabilizes a structure, well-integrated core beliefs provide stability and direction in your life. Stoicism teaches that virtues such as wisdom, courage, justice, and temperance should form the bedrock of your foundation. These aren't just abstract concepts but practical guides that can steer your decisions and interactions. For instance, by embracing Stoic wisdom, you learn to see things as they really are, not as you wish them to be, leading to more realistic and grounded conclusions. Courage in Stoicism isn't just about heroic acts but about everyday bravery, such as standing up for what is right or admitting your mistakes.

Developing a personal ethical code based on Stoic virtues involves more than merely understanding these principles; it requires a commitment to live by them. This can start with small daily decisions—choosing honesty over deceit, patience over impulsiveness, or long-term good over short-term gain. Over time, these choices become habits, reinforcing your ethical code into your identity. Consider creating a personal "virtue manifesto," a written statement of the key Stoic virtues you aspire to live by, tailored to your individual goals and challenges. This manifesto can serve as a constant reminder and guide, helping you align your actions with your ethical framework, especially when faced with moral dilemmas or personal trials.

The beauty of Stoicism lies in its adaptability; it recognizes that life is diverse and ever-changing, and it allows for the flexibility to interpret its principles according to individual circumstances. This flexibility is crucial because it acknowledges that each person's life journey is unique. For example, the way you practice Stoic justice may seem different if you're a teacher, a parent, or a business leader, but the underlying principle—acting with fairness and consideration for others—remains the same. This adaptability urges you to personalize Stoic wisdom, making it relevant and applicable to your specific life situations, whether you're navigating career changes, personal relationships, or internal conflicts.

The transformative power of adopting a Stoic life philosophy is profound—it's about more than just coping with life's challenges; it's about thriving despite them. Stoicism equips you with tools to maintain inner peace in chaos, see growth in challenges, and foster harmony in relationships. It encourages a proactive approach to life, where you're not merely reacting to events but actively shaping your responses in line with your values. This proactive stance is empowering, instilling a sense of control and satisfaction that permeates all areas of life. As you continue to live out Stoic principles, you'll likely notice a shift in your overall well-being—a deeper sense of fulfillment, resilience against adversity, and a harmonious alignment with the world around you.

Embracing Stoicism as a life philosophy transforms everyday living into a more intentional and reflective practice, where each choice and action becomes proof of your values and beliefs. It fosters a life of purpose and integrity, where you're not just existing but truly living—guided by wisdom, driven by virtue, and fulfilled by the harmony between your beliefs and your actions. As you weave Stoic principles into the fabric of your life, you create a vibrant tapestry of experiences that not only reflects your true self but also contributes positively to the world around you.

STOICISM FOR LIFE TRANSITIONS AND NEW BEGINNINGS

Life, in its essence, is a series of transitions—each phase ushering in new challenges and opportunities. Whether it's stepping into a new career, moving to a different city, beginning or ending relationships, or other pivotal life events, these changes can be daunting. Stoicism, with its rich reservoir of wisdom, offers not just comfort but practical strategies for navigating these changes with poise and clarity.

Consider the profound impact of embracing Stoic virtues during these transitions. Courage, for instance, is not merely about boldly facing new challenges; it's about the subtle bravery of stepping into the unknown with hopefulness. It's about saying yes to a new job or a move across the country despite the uncertainties. Wisdom, another Stoic virtue, plays a critical role in making sound decisions during these times. It involves thoughtful consideration of the potential long-term effects of your choices, ensuring that your decisions align with your deepest values and long-term goals. Temperance, or the moderation of your desires and impulses, ensures that you maintain balance amidst the upheaval of change, preventing extreme reactions that might lead to regret.

The practical application of these principles is straightforward yet profound. For example, as you approach a significant career change, employ Stoic wisdom by thoroughly evaluating the new opportunity. Consider not only the financial and professional benefits but also how this change aligns with your values and long-term ambitions. Use temperance to balance your excitement with practicality, ensuring that your decision is well-rounded and sustainable. And let courage motivate you to take this step forward, even if it means leaving your comfort zone.

Strategies for Embracing New Beginnings with a Stoic Mindset

Adopting a Stoic mindset can be incredibly beneficial In effectively managing the uncertainties of new beginnings. Start by envisioning these changes as opportunities for growth rather than obstacles. This shift in perspective can significantly reduce anxiety and increase your openness to new experiences. Practically, this might involve setting clear, achievable goals for the transition period. For instance, if you are relocating, one of your goals could be to explore and connect with the community, which not only helps you to adapt to the new environment but also build a support system.

Another strategy is to maintain a Stoic journal during transitions. Regular entries allow you to reflect on your experiences, monitor your emotional and mental state, and assess how well you're aligning your actions with Stoic virtues. This practice not only provides clarity and direction but also serves as a record of your growth and adaptation through important life changes.

Stories of Stoic Adaptation

The practicality of Stoicism in navigating life's transitions is not just theoretical but is vividly illustrated in the lives of both historical and contemporary figures. Consider the story of Cato the Younger, a Roman politician known for his Stoic virtues. Facing the tumultuous political landscape of his time and the rise of Julius Caesar, Cato remained steadfast in his principles, demonstrating immense courage and integrity. His life serves as a profound example of how Stoic virtues can guide us through personal and societal upheavals.

In more recent times, consider the story of a modern executive who, after a sudden industry shift, found herself contemplating a significant career change. By applying Stoic principles, she navigated this transition with grace and foresight. She used wisdom to evaluate her options, courage to eventually start her consultancy, and temperance to maintain balance during the initial unstable months. Her success today is not just about her professional achievements but about her ability to maintain peace and satisfaction through life's unpredictable waves.

These stories not only inspire us but also demonstrate that Stoicism is as applicable in today's dynamic world as it was in ancient times. They show that Stoicism provides more than just a philosophical comfort; it offers practical tools that can help us navigate life's inevitable changes with confidence and wisdom.

Transitioning through life's various phases can indeed be challenging, but with Stoic principles as your guide, these become less about survival and more about flourishing. By embracing the virtues of courage, wisdom, and temperance and by viewing each change as an opportunity for growth, you equip yourself to handle new beginnings with a calm and optimistic mindset. This approach not only enhances your immediate adaptation but also contributes to a life of rich and fulfilling experiences marked by personal growth and resilience.

As we close this exploration of Stoicism for life transitions and new beginnings, remember that each change you face is not just a test of your ability to adapt but an opportunity to deepen your practice of Stoic virtues. These principles don't merely help you navigate changes; they transform how you experience them, turning each transition into a stepping stone towards a more virtuous and fulfilling life.

In the next chapter, we will explore how to maintain and deepen your Stoic practice over the long term, ensuring that Stoicism remains a vibrant and compelling part of your everyday life.

12

STOICISM IN THE DIGITAL AGE

In an era where the buzz of notifications and the glow of screens dominate much of our waking hours, how do we reclaim our attention and use our digital tools to enhance rather than detract from our lives? The ancient Stoics, who valued mastery over one's mind and impulses, offer a surprisingly relevant guide for navigating our modern digital landscape. This chapter will explore how you can apply Stoic discipline to handle digital distractions and enhance your focus, productivity, and peace of mind.

MANAGING DIGITAL DISTRACTIONS THROUGH STOIC DISCIPLINE

It is no secret that our digital devices, while incredibly useful, can also be sources of constant distraction. Social media notifications, the lure of endlessly scrolling through news feeds, and the rapid influx of emails can fragment our attention and lessen our ability to focus on the tasks and moments that truly matter. The challenge, then, is not just to use technology but to use it wisely and well.

The Stoic Principle of Control

Stoicism teaches us to distinguish between what we can control and what we cannot. In the context of digital distractions, this means recognizing that while we cannot control the design of apps or the strategies tech companies use to capture our attention, we can control our responses to these technologies. We have the power to choose where to direct our attention. This realization is the first step in reclaiming control over our digital interactions.

One effective Stoic exercise to enhance this aspect of control involves setting intentional times for checking emails or social media. For instance, rather than reacting to notifications as they arrive, you might decide to check your email only at set times during the day—perhaps once in the morning, once after lunch, and once before the end of your workday. This practice not only reduces the fragmentation of your attention but also allows you to engage with digital content more deliberately and effectively.

Creating a Disciplined Digital Environment

To further support your Stoic discipline in the digital realm, consider the physical and virtual environments in which you interact with technology. Decluttering your digital spaces can have a profound impact on your mental clarity and ability to focus. Start by organizing your digital files and uninstalling apps that you no longer use, or that tend to waste your time. Utilize technology tools that limit usage or block distracting websites during work hours to help maintain your focus.

Additionally, creating physical boundaries for device use can be incredibly helpful. Designate specific areas of your home, such as the bedroom or dining room, as tech-free zones. This not only helps reduce digital distractions but also promotes better sleep and more meaningful interactions with family members.

Stoic Mindfulness in Digital Engagements

Another powerful Stoic practice involves using moments of digital engagement as opportunities to practice self-control and mindfulness. Before opening an app or responding to an email, take a moment to breathe deeply and remind yourself of your intention for this interaction. Ask yourself: Is this action necessary? Is it aligned with my values and goals? By pausing to reflect in this way, you transform a potentially mindless reaction into a mindful action.

Visual Element: The Stoic Digital Discipline Flowchart

To aid in applying these principles, consider the Stoic Digital Discipline Flowchart—an infographic that outlines a step-by-step process to manage digital distractions effectively. This flowchart prompts you to ask key questions before engaging with digital technology, helping you make more deliberate and controlled use of your devices. It serves as a visual reminder of the Stoic principles discussed in this section, integrating ancient wisdom with modern challenges to help you navigate your digital life with greater purpose and tranquility.

SOCIAL MEDIA AND STOICISM: MAINTAINING EMOTIONAL EQUANIMITY ONLINE

In the vast, interconnected web of social media, it's easy to fall into the trap of constant comparison, where every post and update from others can seem like a reflection of what we lack. This digital landscape, brimming with curated realities showcasing perfect lives, can significantly skew our perception, leading to feelings of inadequacy, envy, or even anger. Yet, through the lens of Stoicism, we find valuable strategies to navigate this space more mindfully, ensuring that our engagement with social media enriches rather than depletes us.

Stoic Wisdom on Emotional Detachment

The Stoic practice of emotional detachment offers a powerful antidote to the negative impacts of social media. By focusing on internal values rather than external validation, Stoicism teaches us to cultivate indifference to things that lie outside our moral purpose. This doesn't mean we should adopt a callous or disconnected attitude; instead, we should choose to anchor our self-worth in our own virtues and actions rather than in the approval of others. For instance, when encountering a post that triggers feelings of jealousy or inadequacy, a Stoic approach would involve a conscious shift of focus from external measures of success—like wealth or physical appearance—to personal progress and ethical integrity. This shift not only alleviates distressing emotions but also aligns our social media interactions with our deeper values, fostering a sense of contentment and self-respect.

Mindful Engagement with Social Media

To further enhance our experience online, Stoicism encourages the practice of mindfulness, particularly in how we engage with social media. This involves being acutely aware of our emotional state before, during, and after our digital interactions. By examining ourselves prior to scrolling through social media, we can better understand our motivations—are we seeking connection, distraction, or validation? During our engagement, maintaining this awareness helps us notice when feelings of distress or comparison begin to surface, allowing us to pause and realign with our Stoic principles. Afterward, reflecting on our feelings can inform whether our interaction was beneficial or if adjustments are needed in our future engagements. This mindful approach transforms our social media use from a passive and potentially harmful activity into an opportunity for personal growth and self-awareness.

Stoic Reflections on Social Media Interactions

Regular reflection on our interactions with social media is a critical Stoic practice that can significantly enhance our online experiences. By taking time to assess whether our engagements are contributing positively to our lives, we can make informed decisions about how best to use these powerful tools. This might involve setting boundaries around the time spent online, curating our feeds to include more positive and inspiring content, or even taking periodic breaks from social media to reconnect with our offline lives. Such reflections not only help in maintaining emotional balance but also ensure that our digital habits align with our overall goals and values, reinforcing our Stoic commitment to living a virtuous life.

In practicing these Stoic strategies—emotional detachment, mindful engagement, and regular reflection—we not only protect ourselves from the potential downsides of social media but also harness its capabilities to support our personal and spiritual growth. These practices empower us to navigate the digital realm with wisdom and composure, turning every scroll or click into a step toward greater self-understanding and equanimity.

APPLYING STOICISM TO ONLINE INTERACTIONS AND RELATIONSHIPS

In the vast expanse of the digital world, our interactions often lack the physical and emotional cues that guide our communications in person. This absence can sometimes lead to less empathetic and more impulsive exchanges, where the anonymity and physical detachment of online platforms may encourage behaviors and statements that we might shy away from in face-to-face settings. The veil of a screen can embolden some to express harsher criticisms or engage in more confrontational dialogue than they usually would. Understanding these dynamics is crucial in applying Stoic principles to navigate online environments effectively.

The Stoic virtues—justice, temperance, and courage—are not just ideals for personal development but are immensely practical in enhancing online interactions. Justice, in a Stoic sense, involves treating others fairly and with kindness, an approach that is often challenged in the faceless interactions of the internet. To embody Stoic justice online, remember that behind every profile picture and username is an actual person with real feelings, challenges, and a life as complex as your own. This understanding can temper our responses, ensuring they are not just truthful but also considerate and constructive.

Temperance, or moderation, is another virtue that is vital in the digital realm. It guides us to respond to others—not with impulsive reactions—but with measured, thoughtful words. Applying temperance can mean taking a moment to breathe and reflect before replying to a provocative comment or choosing not to engage in every debate you encounter online. This not only helps maintain your peace of mind but also fosters a more constructive online environment. For instance, if you experience a heated debate within a social media group, choosing to provide a balanced, well-thought-out response, or sometimes choosing not to engage at all, can be a demonstration of temperance.

The virtue of courage, which in Stoicism involves not just bravery in the face of physical danger but also the moral courage to speak and live truthfully, is particularly relevant when we consider the spread of misinformation online. Exhibiting Stoic courage can mean standing up for truth and integrity by fact-checking information before sharing it or by respectfully correcting misconceptions in online discussions. It requires bravery to maintain your ethical standards even when it might be easier or more comfortable to blend into the consensus and stay silent.

Guidelines for Virtuous Online Behavior

It's helpful to establish clear personal guidelines rooted in Stoic virtues in order to maintain decorum and respect in online discussions, especially when faced with challenging interactions such as dealing with internet trolls. First, always aim to communicate with respect and sincerity, keeping in mind that your words have the power to affect others deeply. When encountering trolls or overly aggressive commenters, a Stoic approach would involve responding with calmness and logic or choosing not to engage at all, thereby not allowing such interactions to disturb your peace.

Creating a positive impact in digital communities can also involve actively contributing to discussions that foster understanding and shared learning. Share insights, offer support, and express appreciation for valuable contributions from others. These actions not only enrich the community but also strengthen your practice of Stoic virtues by focusing on constructive and meaningful exchanges.

Moreover, the role of community in Stoicism is profoundly significant. Modern online platforms can serve as contemporary Stoic communities where individuals seek advice, find support, and share wisdom. Participating in or even forming online groups focused on Stoic philosophy and its application in daily life can provide valuable opportunities for learning and growth. These communities allow for the exchange of ideas and experiences that can deepen understanding and inspire the practical application of Stoic principles in diverse aspects of life.

Navigating the digital world through the lens of Stoicism equips you not only to handle the challenges of online interactions but to transform these experiences into opportunities for personal growth and positive contributions. The practice of these ancient virtues on modern platforms demonstrates the timeless relevance of Stoic wisdom, guiding us to lead more thoughtful, balanced, and meaningful digital lives.

THE MODERN STOIC: INTEGRATING ANCIENT WISDOM IN A HIGH-TECH WORLD

In an age where technology permeates every aspect of our lives, the challenge often lies not in adopting new technologies but in integrating them in ways that enhance our well-being rather than detract from it. The ancient practice of Stoicism, with its focus on wisdom, virtue, and self-control, offers valuable insights into how we can use modern technologies, such as digital apps and virtual reality, to deepen our understanding and practice of these timeless principles.

The adaptation of traditional Stoic practices, such as journaling and meditation, to modern technologies is not just a matter of convenience but also enhances accessibility and engagement. For instance, digital journaling apps can ease the Stoic practice of daily reflection by making it easier to track thoughts, emotions, and actions over time. These apps often come with features like reminders and prompts, which can help you maintain consistency in your reflective practices. Similarly, virtual reality offers new dimensions to meditation, allowing you to immerse yourself in serene environments that might not be manageable in your daily surroundings. This can be particularly beneficial in cultivating the Stoic practice of mindfulness and presence, as these immersive experiences can help you detach from everyday distractions and focus intensely on your internal state.

Moreover, the benefits of technology in practicing Stoicism also extend to educational and community aspects. Many apps are dedicated to Stoicism and provide daily meditations, quotes from Stoic philosophers, and interactive exercises that make the philosophy more accessible and applicable to everyday life. These digital platforms not only serve as tools for individual practice but also foster a sense of community among those interested in Stoicism. Users can share insights, discuss interpretations of Stoic texts, and support each other in applying Stoic principles to modern challenges. This communal aspect is crucial, as Stoicism emphasizes not only personal growth but also the development of virtues that contribute to the welfare of society.

However, the incorporation of Stoicism into our high-tech world is not without its challenges. The rapid pace of digital interactions and the often superficial nature of online communications can seem at odds with the profound, reflective nature of Stoic philosophy. Here, the Stoic practice of mindfulness becomes especially relevant. By consciously slowing down our interactions with technology—pausing to reflect on the purpose and impact of our digital engagements—we can counteract the frenetic pace of the digital age. This might involve setting intentions before using technology, such as seeking to learn something new or connecting meaningfully with others rather than mindlessly scrolling through content.

Encouraging a balanced approach to technology is also essential. Stoicism teaches us to use external things without becoming dependent on them, a principle that can guide our use of technology. It's about leveraging technology to enhance our lives and virtues without letting it dictate our happiness or self-worth. For example, while a Stoic app might help you practice mindfulness, it's essential also to cultivate the ability to be mindful without it, ensuring that your practice is grounded in internal skills rather than external aids.

In embracing these strategies, you align with the Stoic ideal of living according to nature. In today's terms, this can be interpreted as living in harmony with the technological environment that surrounds us—using it thoughtfully and purposefully to enhance our capacity for virtue, wisdom, and contentment. By doing so, you not only navigate the high-tech world more effectively but also deepen your practice of Stoicism, finding in ancient wisdom a powerful partner for modern living.

As we conclude this exploration of integrating Stoicism in the digital age, we see how ancient practices can find new expressions and applications in modern settings. This chapter has shown that by adapting Stoic wisdom to contemporary tools, we can enhance our understanding and application of this philosophical tradition, making it even more relevant and valuable in our daily lives. The next chapter will focus on consolidating these practices into a cohesive Stoic lifestyle, ensuring that the principles of Stoicism are not just something we study but something we live, day by day.

CONCLUSION

As we draw the curtains on this journey through the enriching landscape of Stoicism, it's essential to reflect on the transformative power this ancient philosophy holds for our modern lives. Stoicism isn't merely a set of theories confined to dusty old tomes; it's a vibrant, practical guide that offers enduring wisdom for navigating today's world with its rapid changes, overwhelming choices, and unprecedented challenges.

Throughout this book, we've explored how Stoicism can help us manage stress, engage more mindfully with technology, cultivate robust relationships, and foster personal growth. Each chapter has not only delved into Stoic principles but has also connected these age-old ideas to contemporary issues—whether in dealing with digital distractions, enhancing emotional intelligence, or navigating complex social dynamics.

Key Takeaways: Remember, adopting Stoicism is about more than understanding its philosophy; it's about living it. The core Stoic virtues—wisdom, courage, justice, and temperance—can guide your daily decisions and interactions. By practicing mindfulness, engaging in daily reflections, and approaching life's challenges with a Stoic mindset, you can cultivate a life of peace, resilience, and fulfillment.

Call to Action: I urge you, the reader, to not view this as the end but as the beginning of your Stoic practice. Start with small, manageable steps. Integrate moments of reflection into your morning routine, practice mindfulness throughout your day, and challenge yourself to respond to life's complexities with Stoic calm and rationality. These practices are not meant to be temporary fixes but parts of a lifelong journey toward more profound wisdom and greater virtue.

Join the Stoic Community: You are not alone on this path. The Stoic community, both online and possibly in your local area, offers a network of support and friendship. Engage with forums, participate in discussions, and attend Stoic meetings and events. Sharing your journey with others can provide not only inspiration but also fresh perspectives that enrich your understanding of Stoicism.

Encourage Personal Exploration: I urge you to dive deeper into the texts of Marcus Aurelius, Seneca, and Epictetus, among others. Each Stoic philosopher offers unique insights that you might find resonate differently with your personal experiences and challenges. Remember, Stoicism is highly personal, and its application can be tailored to fit your individual life circumstances and values.

Acknowledge the Ongoing Nature of Stoic Practice: Embrace the fact that Stoicism is a path, not a destination. It is a philosophy of ongoing practice and continual growth. There will be setbacks and challenges, but each is an opportunity to apply Stoic principles and learn from the experience.

Finally, I want to express my heartfelt gratitude to you for joining me in exploring the profound and practical world of Stoicism. May this book serve as a steadfast companion as you navigate the complexities of modern life. Approach each day with Stoic wisdom and serenity, and remember that every moment is an opportunity to live according to your highest virtues.

Thank you for embarking on this journey towards a Stoic life. May you find in Stoicism the strength, peace, and joy that I have discovered.

REFERENCES

What is Stoicism? The Basics of The World's Greatest ... https://orionphilosophy.com/stoicism-meaning-and-definition/

Zeno of Citium | Stoic, Cynic, Founder https://www.britannica.com/biography/Zeno-of-Citium

Mastering Modern Life with Stoic Philosophy: 10 Insights and ... https://thegeekyleader.com/2024/01/07/mastering-modern-life-with-stoic-philosophy-10-insights-and-practical-applications/

How to be a Modern Stoic: Stoicism in the 21st Century https://mindandpractice.com/how-to-be-a-modern-stoic-stoicism-in-the-21st-century/

Best Quotes from Seneca's Letters from a Stoic https://www.getstoic.com/quotes/best-quotes-seneca-letters-from-a-stoic/

How To Plan Your Day Like Marcus Aurelius https://dailystoic.com/marcus-aurelius-daily-habits/

Epictetus on Freedom, Thinking, Information and ... https://fs.blog/the-art-of-living/

Why Stoicism Is More Relevant Than You Might Think https://www.psychologytoday.com/us/blog/365-ways-to-be-more-stoic/202301/why-stoicism-is-more-relevant-than-you-might-think/

Beginners Guide to Stoicism https://modernstoicism.com/beginners-guide-to-stoicism/

Modern Stoicism: How To Use Ancient ... https://orionphilosophy.com/stoic-philosophy-for-modern-life/

A Stoic's 9-Minute Micro Morning Routine For Guaranteed ... https://medium.com/mind-cafe/a-stoics-9-minute-micro-morning-routine-a86e87e7101d/

Resilience: Build skills to endure hardship https://www.mayoclinic.org/tests-procedures/resilience-training/in-depth/resilience/art-20046311/

The Stoic Dichotomy of Control in Practice https://www.psychologytoday.com/us/blog/365-ways-to-be-more-stoic/202304/the-stoic-dichotomy-of-control-in-practice/

Cognitive Restructuring Techniques for Reframing Thoughts https://positivepsychology.com/cbt-cognitive-restructuring-cognitive-distortions/

21 Mindfulness Exercises & Activities For Adults (+ PDF) https://positivepsychology.com/mindfulness-exercises-techniques-activities/

Famous Stoics in History and Pop Culture | Living By Example https://www.livingbyexample.org/famous-stoics-in-history-and-pop-culture/

Stoicism for Conflict Resolution: Use Stoic Philosophy to ... https://www.stoicsimple. com/stoicism-for-conflict-resolution-use-stoic-philosophy-to-resolve-conflicts/

What Stoic Philosophy Says About Love | by Wesley Owens https://medium.com/ love-the-magazine/what-stoic-philosophy-says-about-love-913bb82c416d/

Communication & Stoicism: How to Communicate Better with Stoic Philosophy https://www.stoicsimple.com/communication-stoicism-how-to-communicate-better-with-stoic-philosophy/

Stoic advice: what do Stoics think of forgiveness? https://howtobeastoic.wordpress. com/2017/04/22/stoic-advice-what-do-stoics-think-of-forgiveness/

How to Let Go of Anger: Seneca's 16 Stoic Techniques https://www.highexistence. com/seneca-on-how-to-deal-with-anger/

Stoicism and Envy: Using Stoic Philosophy to Deal With ... https://www.stoicsimple. com/stoicism-and-envy-using-stoic-philosophy-to-deal-with-jealousy/

How to Cope With Fear and Anxiety, the Stoic Way https://www.psychologytoday. com/us/blog/hide-and-seek/202203/how-to-cope-with-fear-and-anxiety-the-stoic-way/

Benefits Of Adopting A Stoic Mindset In Your Work And Life https://www.forbes. com/sites/jackkelly/2024/04/12/benefits-of-stoicism/

A Stoic Response to Grief https://dailystoic.com/stoic-response-grief/

The Stoic Resilience of James Stockdale - The Will Project https://willproject.org/ examples/stoic-resilience-stockdale/

How Stoicism Perfectly Helps You Deal With Change https://orionphilosophy.com/ stoicism-change/

MODERN STOICISM AND ITS USEFULNESS IN ... https://www.crisisjournal.org/ api/v1/articles/33608-modern-stoicism-and-its-usefulness-in-fostering-resilience.pdf/

Cognitive Behavior Therapy - StatPearls https://www.ncbi.nlm.nih.gov/books/ NBK470241/

Mindfulness exercises - Mayo Clinic https://www.mayoclinic.org/healthy-lifestyle/ consumer-health/in-depth/mindfulness-exercises/art-20046356/

The empirical status of acceptance and commitment therapy https://www. sciencedirect.com/science/article/pii/S2212144720301940

Road to resilience: a systematic review and meta-analysis ... https://bmjopen.bmj. com/content/8/6/e017858/

Eudaimonia https://www.thestoicregistry.org/res/pathways/eudaimonia/

Stoicism vs. Hedonism: What's the Difference? https://orionphilosophy.com/ stoicism-vs-hedonism/

10 Insanely Useful Stoic Exercises https://dailystoic.com/10-insanely-useful-stoic-exercises/

5 Epic Leaders Who Studied Stoicism -- and Why You ... https://www.entrepreneur.

com/leadership/5-epic-leaders-who-studied-stoicism-and-why-you-should/252625/

The Stoic Paradoxes - Stoic Compass - WordPress.com https://stoiccompass.wordpress.com/2017/10/20/the-stoic-paradoxes/

An Ancient Stoic Meditation Technique https://donaldrobertson.name/2017/03/22/an-ancient-stoic-meditation-technique/

6 Stoicism and Modern Virtue Ethics - Oxford Academic https://academic.oup.com/book/44871/chapter/384583553/

10 Stoic Habits for Maintaining Work-Life Balance https://thegeekyleader.com/2024/05/26/10-stoic-habits-for-maintaining-work-life-balance/

How To Practice Stoicism: An Introduction & 12 ... https://mindfulstoic.net/how-to-practice-stoicism-an-introduction-12-stoic-practices/

A Daily Regimen for the Modern Stoic | by PocketStoic Staff https://medium.com/pocketstoic/a-daily-regimen-for-the-modern-stoic-e4b9ae750e58/

The Modern Application of Stoic Philosophy in Daily Life https://stoicstateuniversity.com/blog/the-modern-application-of-stoic-philosophy-in-daily-life/

How Stoicism Perfectly Helps You Deal With Change https://orionphilosophy.com/stoicism-change/

Stoic Principles in the Digital Age: A Guide to Digital Detox https://medium.com/@m.daudup25/stoic-principles-in-the-digital-age-a-guide-to-digital-detox-aed25905b650/

The Stoics were right – emotional control is good for the soul https://psyche.co/ideas/the-stoics-were-right-emotional-control-is-good-for-the-soul/

Managing Social Media Stress with Mindfulness https://childmind.org/article/social-media-stress-mindfulness/

A Daily Regimen for the Modern Stoic | by PocketStoic Staff https://medium.com/pocketstoic/a-daily-regimen-for-the-modern-stoic-e4b9ae750e58/

THE PHILOSOPHY OF STOICISM

ADVANCED STOIC TECHNIQUES FOR BUILDING RESILIENCE, INNER PEACE, AND WISDOM

INTRODUCTION

Many years ago, I found myself at a crossroads. Life was moving fast, and the pressures of work and personal commitments seemed overwhelming. One day, while browsing a bookstore, I stumbled upon a worn-out copy of Marcus Aurelius's book, *Meditations*. Intrigued by the idea of a Roman Emperor reflecting on life, I bought the book. Little did I know this would start a transformative journey into Stoicism.

My book aims to offer you the same kind of transformation. Its purpose is to provide a guide to mastering advanced Stoic philosophy and practices. Stoicism is not just an ancient philosophy but a practical approach to living a balanced and meaningful life in our chaotic world. It teaches us to face challenges with wisdom, strength, and peace of mind.

This book is targeted at adults who are seeking to navigate life's challenges more effectively. Whether you are a professional striving for balance, a self-improvement enthusiast, or simply curious about philosophy, this book has something to offer. Stoicism speaks to the universal human experience—our struggles, resilience, and quest for meaning.

The structure of this is designed to be both comprehensive and practical. We will start by exploring advanced Stoic principles like virtue ethics and the dichotomy of control. Then, we will move into practical exercises for building emotional resilience, including cognitive reframing and *premeditatio malorum*. Daily meditation, reflection, and journaling practices will be covered to help you internalize Stoic teachings. Finally, we will discuss applying Stoicism to contemporary issues such as stress management and uncertainty.

What can you expect to gain from this book? First, you will develop emotional resilience. Life will still throw challenges your way, but you will be better equipped to handle them. You will also find inner peace, even amid chaos. Your decision-making will improve as you learn to focus on what you can control and let go of what you cannot, and personal growth will follow as you commit to a lifelong journey of self-improvement and wisdom.

The insights in this book are backed by extensive research. I have drawn from ancient texts, modern academic papers, and my experiences. My background as a scholar of philosophy and my years of studying Stoicism add credibility to the content. This is not just theory; it is a practical guide grounded in ancient wisdom and modern research.

By the end of this book, you will have a toolkit of practical, actionable guidance that you can integrate into your daily life. You will be able to face life's challenges with a new perspective and a sense of calm. The aim is not just to read about Stoicism but to live it.

I encourage you to engage with the content actively. Each chapter includes exercises, reflection questions, and journaling prompts to help you internalize and apply Stoic principles. Keep an open mind and commit to practicing these techniques. The more you engage, the more you will benefit.

As we embark on this journey together, remember that the path to wisdom and resilience is lifelong. There will be moments of challenge and moments of triumph. Through it all, Stoicism will be your guide. It will help you navigate the complexities of life with clarity and strength.

So, let's begin this journey. Let's explore the rich tapestry of Stoic wisdom and uncover how it can change our lives. The road ahead promises not just knowledge but profound, lasting change. Welcome to a life guided by Stoic principles.

1

FOUNDATIONS OF ADVANCED STOIC PHILOSOPHY

One evening, after a particularly grueling day at work, I found myself reflecting on the chaos and stress that seemed to dominate my life. I had been reading about Stoicism and was struck by a passage from Marcus Aurelius's *Meditations*. This Stoic philosopher wrote, "You have power over your mind—not outside events. Realize this, and you will find strength." This simple yet profound idea resonated deeply, and I began seeing the world differently. It was the first step in my journey toward understanding and applying Stoic philosophy.

In this chapter, we will explore the bedrock of Stoic philosophy: virtue ethics. We will delve into virtue, which, according to Stoicism, is life's highest good and ultimate aim. We will discuss the role of reason and rationality in achieving virtue and the belief in the universality of virtue. Practical exercises will be provided to help you cultivate virtue in your daily life.

VIRTUE ETHICS: THE CORE OF STOICISM

At the heart of Stoic philosophy lies the concept of virtue ethics. According to the Stoics, virtue is life's highest good and ultimate aim. Unlike other ethical systems prioritizing happiness or pleasure, Stoicism places virtue above all else. Virtue ethics is about developing a moral character and living according to nature. This means understanding and accepting the natural order of things and acting in a way that aligns with it. The Stoics believed that we can achieve a life of true contentment and purpose by cultivating virtues such as wisdom, courage, justice, and moderation.

Reason and rationality play a crucial role in achieving virtue. The Stoics thought that humans are rational beings and that our reasoning ability sets us apart from other animals. Using reason, we can understand the world and make moral decisions that align with nature. One of the most well-known Stoic philosophers, Marcus Aurelius, often reflected on the importance of rational thinking. He wrote in *Meditations*, "The happiness of your life depends upon the quality of your thoughts." He also emphasized the need for rational decision-making processes. By evaluating our actions and their consequences logically, we can ensure that we act virtuously.

The Stoic belief in the universality of virtue is another crucial aspect of their philosophy. The Stoics believed that virtue is accessible to everyone, regardless of social status or wealth. As one of the most prominent Stoic philosophers, Seneca often wrote in his letters about the equality of all humans in their capacity for virtue. He stated, "Virtue is that which is honorable and becoming, and is of profit to the possessor." This egalitarian principle is reflected in modern views on equality and justice. Everyone has the potential to cultivate virtue, and it is through our actions and choices that we demonstrate our moral character.

Practical Exercises to Develop Virtue Daily

Practical exercises are essential to help you develop virtue in your daily life. Begin by incorporating daily journaling prompts that encourage self-reflection. For instance, at the end of each day, write about a situation where you acted virtuously or could have acted more virtuously. Reflect on your actions and intentions, and think about how to improve. Another exercise is to ask yourself reflective questions throughout the day. When you have a choice, ask, Is this aligned with virtue? Am I doing this out of wisdom, courage, justice, or moderation? These questions guide you toward making more ethical choices.

When you understand and apply these virtue ethics principles, you will see positive change in your life. You will find that true contentment comes not from external circumstances but from living by your values and principles. This foundation of Stoic philosophy will serve as a guide as we explore more advanced techniques and practices in the chapters to come.

THE FOUR CARDINAL VIRTUES: WISDOM, JUSTICE, COURAGE, AND MODERATION

In Stoicism, the four cardinal virtues—Wisdom, Justice, Courage, and Moderation—form the backbone of ethical living. These virtues are not mere abstract concepts but practical guides for navigating life's complexities. Each virtue has its roots in the ancient philosophical tradition. Yet their relevance remains undiminished in modern times. Wisdom, or "Sophia," is the ability to make sound judgments and understand the world through reason. Justice, or "Dikaiosyne," emphasizes fairness and moral integrity in our interactions. Courage, or "Andreia," involves facing challenges with bravery. Moderation, or "Sophrosyne," advocates for balance and self-control in all aspects of life. These virtues collectively lead to a life of moral excellence and inner peace.

Wisdom (Sophia) is the cornerstone of Stoic philosophy. It involves discerning the right course of action in any given situation. Stoics believe that wisdom is achieved through the constant pursuit of knowledge and self-reflection. In *Meditations*, Marcus Aurelius often pondered the essence of wisdom. He wrote, "The object of life is not to be on the side of the majority, but to escape finding oneself in the ranks of the insane." This quote underscores the importance of independent, rational thought. In daily life, practical wisdom can manifest in various ways. For example, when faced with a difficult decision at work, gathering all relevant information and considering the long-term consequences aligns with the Stoic virtue of wisdom. It means not acting impulsively but thoughtfully ensuring our actions are grounded in reason and ethical principles.

Justice (Dikaiosyne) is another critical virtue in Stoicism. It is about treating others fairly and acting with moral integrity. Seneca's writings often highlight the significance of justice. In his letters, he stated, "Treat your inferiors as you would be treated by your superiors." This principle of reciprocity is fundamental to Stoic justice. In modern contexts, justice can be seen in actions that promote equality and fairness. For example, advocating for fair treatment of all employees in a workplace or standing up against discrimination reflects the Stoic commitment to justice. These actions uphold moral integrity and contribute to a more equitable society. Embodying justice ensures that our interactions are fair and contribute positively to our communities.

The Stoic virtue of Courage (Andreia) is essential for facing life's inevitable challenges. Stoics view courage as the strength to confront fear, pain, and adversity. It is about standing firm in the face of difficulties and maintaining moral integrity even when challenging. Personal stories of courage abound in Stoic literature. Consider the tale of Epictetus, one of the most renowned Stoic philosophers. He was born into slavery and endured physical suffering but remained steadfast in his philosophical convictions. His courage in adversity serves as an inspiration for us all. We can start with small acts of courage in our daily lives to cultivate bravery. Facing a problematic conversation head-on, standing up for what is right, or pushing through a challenging project at work are all ways to practice courage. These actions build our resilience and prepare us to face more considerable challenges with a Stoic mindset.

Moderation (Sophrosyne) is about finding balance and exercising self-control. It is the virtue that prevents excess and ensures that we live in harmony with our values and principles. The Stoics believed that moderation is crucial for maintaining physical and mental well-being. Practical tips for practicing moderation include limiting indulgences, whether in food, drink, or even work. For instance, having a balanced diet, regular exercise, and ensuring adequate rest are all ways to practice moderation. In ancient contexts, Stoics like Musonius Rufus, another prominent Stoic philosopher, emphasized moderation in all aspects of life, advising against excess and deficiency. This might translate to finding a healthy work-life balance in modern times, where neither work nor leisure is neglected. Practicing moderation creates a balanced life that aligns with our values and promotes long-term well-being.

By consistently practicing these four cardinal virtues, we can achieve a life of moral excellence and inner peace. Each virtue—Wisdom, Justice, Courage, and Moderation—guides our actions and decisions, ensuring that we live according to our highest principles. As we continue exploring Stoic philosophy, these virtues will serve as a base for understanding and applying Stoic teachings.

THE DICHOTOMY OF CONTROL: WHAT YOU CAN AND CANNOT CONTROL

A fundamental Stoic principle is the "dichotomy of control." It offers a straightforward, practical approach to many of life's uncertainties. This principle is rooted in the teachings of Epictetus. He asserted that some things are within our control while others are not. We gain mental peace and resilience by focusing on the factors we can influence and accepting those we cannot. Epictetus famously stated, "Some things are up to us and some things are not up to us." This simple yet profound distinction lies at the heart of Stoic thought, reminding us to direct our efforts where they will be most effective.

The dichotomy of control differentiates between internal and external factors. Internal factors include our thoughts, actions, desires, and aversions—essentially, everything that originates from within us. External factors encompass everything outside our control, such as other people's actions, external events, and circumstances. For instance, you can control your reaction to a colleague's criticism but not the criticism itself. This distinction has practical applications in modern life and not just theoretical ones. Focusing on our internal responses allows us to navigate external challenges more effectively and with better composure.

Understanding what we can control and cannot is crucial for maintaining mental peace. When we focus on controllable aspects, we reduce stress and anxiety. Take a busy professional facing a tight deadline. They cannot control their boss's workload or expectations, but they can choose their approach to the task, time management, and attitude. Concentrating on these controllable elements allows them to manage stress more effectively and perform better. This shift in focus promotes a sense of calm and confidence, even amid challenging circumstances.

Practical Exercises for Practicing the Dichotomy of Control

Practical exercises can be highly beneficial to internalize the principle of the dichotomy of control. One effective exercise is to create a two-column list. On one side, write down things within your control, such as your actions, attitudes, and reactions. Alternatively, list things outside your control, like the weather, other people's opinions, or global events. Reflect on this list daily to reinforce the distinction. Another helpful exercise involves thought experiments. When faced with a stressful situation, pause and ask yourself, "Is this within my control?" If not, focus your energy on what you can influence.

Real-world scenarios also help in practicing this principle. When you are stuck in traffic on your way to an important meeting, you can't control the traffic but can control your response. Instead of getting frustrated, use the time to listen to an educational podcast or practice deep breathing. This shift in focus transforms a potentially stressful situation into a productive one. Similarly, in personal relationships, you cannot control how others behave, but you can control your reactions. By focusing on your responses, you maintain your inner peace and contribute to healthier interactions.

We must emphasize the importance of focusing on what we can control. It empowers us to take ownership of our lives and reduces the emotional burden of worrying about uncontrollable factors. This focus leads to a more resilient mindset, enabling us to face life's challenges with even more fortitude. Whether dealing with professional setbacks, personal conflicts, or everyday annoyances, the dichotomy of control provides a clear framework for maintaining mental peace and resilience. It is a practical tool that, when consistently applied, transforms our approach to life's inevitable ups and downs.

THE STOIC VIEW OF FATE: AMOR FATI AND ACCEPTANCE

Amor fati, or "the love of fate," is a cornerstone of Stoic philosophy that invites us to embrace everything that happens to us, good and bad. This concept, deeply rooted in Stoicism, suggests that we should accept and love our fate. Stoics believed that everything happens for a reason and that every event is necessary for our growth. Marcus Aurelius captured this sentiment beautifully when he wrote, "A blazing fire makes flame and brightness out of everything that is thrown into it." This idea was later echoed by Friedrich Nietzsche, who described *amor fati* as his formula for human greatness, where one wants nothing to be different and loves what is necessary.

The benefits of accepting fate are profound. Acceptance leads to inner peace and reduces resistance to life's inevitable challenges. Consider the case of Viktor Frankl, a Holocaust survivor and psychiatrist who practiced *amor fati* during his time in concentration camps. Frankl found meaning in his suffering, which allowed him to endure unimaginable hardships. By embracing his fate, he discovered a sense of purpose and strength. Psychologically, acceptance helps us avoid the mental turmoil of fighting against what we cannot change. When we accept our circumstances, we free ourselves from the stress and anxiety of constant resistance. This acceptance does not mean we become passive; instead, it empowers us to face our challenges with a clear mind and a resilient spirit.

It is essential to differentiate between fate and fatalism. Accepting fate, or *amor fati*, is not about passivity or resignation. It is about actively engaging with life and making the best of every situation. For instance, an athlete who suffers a career-ending injury can either wallow in despair or embrace their new reality and find new ways to contribute, perhaps by coaching or mentoring young athletes. This proactive acceptance transforms obstacles into opportunities for growth. In modern life, this principle can be applied professionally and personally. Whether dealing with the loss of a job or a relationship, embracing fate allows us to move forward constructively rather than getting stuck in imagining what might have been.

Practical Exercises for Embracing Amor Fati

To practice *amor fati*, start by reflecting on past events with acceptance. Think about a difficult situation you faced and ask yourself how it contributed to your growth. Write about this experience in a journal, focusing on the positive outcomes that emerged from the challenge. This exercise helps reframe your perspective and fosters a sense of gratitude for the lessons learned. Another valuable exercise is visualization. Imagine a future scenario where things do not go as planned. Visualize how you would accept this outcome and your actions to adapt constructively. This mental rehearsal prepares you to face real-life challenges with a mindset of acceptance and resilience.

By embracing *amor fati*, we see every event as a stepping stone toward personal growth. This shift in perspective reduces our resistance to life's challenges and helps us find meaning and purpose in every experience. As we continue to explore Stoic principles, we will see how this attitude of acceptance and proactive engagement with life enriches our understanding and application of Stoicism.

UNDERSTANDING STOIC PHYSICS AND THEOLOGY

Stoic physics and theology are crucial to understanding the natural world and its divine order. The Stoics believed the universe operates according to a rational and purposeful design governed by a divine principle called "Logos." This concept, central to Stoic thought, posits that the universe is a coherent system where every event is interconnected and meaningful. We can trace the development of Stoic physics back to early Greek philosophers such as Heraclitus, who influenced later Stoics like Zeno of Citium, Chrysippus, and Epictetus. These thinkers built upon the idea that the cosmos is an orderly, living organism permeated by reason and purpose.

Logos is a term derived from Greek, meaning "word" or "reason." The Stoics believed Logos is imminent in all things, providing structure and coherence to the cosmos. This divine reason is not an external deity but an intrinsic aspect of the natural world, guiding its processes and ensuring harmony. Marcus Aurelius reflects on this in *Meditations* by stating, "All things are woven together and the common bond is sacred, and scarcely one thing is alien to another. For they are continuous and in sympathy with one another and all things are coordinated and combine to form the same universe." This highlights the Stoic view that everything in the universe is interconnected and part of a greater whole.

The concept of "cosmic sympathy" is also central to Stoic physics. This idea suggests that all parts of the universe are inextricably linked and that changes in one part affect the whole. The Stoics used the metaphor of a vast organism to describe this interconnectedness, where each part functions in harmony with the others. This perspective finds modern parallels in scientific theories such as the Gaia hypothesis, which views Earth as a self-regulating system, and quantum physics, which reveals the interdependence of particles across vast distances. These scientific parallels affirm the Stoic belief in the interconnectedness of all things, emphasizing that our actions have far-reaching consequences.

Stoic physics and theology remain relevant in contemporary discussions of science and philosophy. The Stoic understanding of the natural world as an interconnected system resonates with modern ecological and environmental ethics. Recognizing the interdependence of all life forms encourages a sense of responsibility toward the environment. For instance, the ethical implications of this view are evident in the principles of sustainability and conservation, which aim to protect the delicate balance of our ecosystems. The Stoic emphasis on living in harmony with nature aligns with contemporary efforts to address climate change and promote environmental stewardship.

In modern physics and cosmology, the Stoic idea of Logos echoes in the search for a unified theory that explains the universe's fundamental forces. Scientists strive to understand the principles governing the cosmos, much like the Stoics sought to comprehend the divine reason that orders everything. This pursuit of knowledge reflects the Stoic commitment to rational inquiry and intellectual curiosity. By relating Stoic physics to contemporary scientific endeavors, we can appreciate the timeless relevance of Stoic thought and its contributions to our understanding of the universe.

The ethical implications of Stoic physics and theology extend beyond environmentalism. They also shape our moral responsibilities toward one another. Believing in cosmic sympathy encourages us to recognize our fates' interconnectedness and shared humanity. This perspective fosters empathy, compassion, and a sense of social responsibility. In a world where individual actions have global repercussions, the Stoic view of interconnectedness reminds us that our choices matter and that we are part of a larger, interdependent community.

STOICISM AND COGNITIVE BEHAVIORAL THERAPY (CBT): A MODERN CONNECTION

In our exploration of Stoic philosophy, it is fascinating to note its profound influence on modern cognitive behavioral therapy (CBT).

This connection is not just historical but deeply practical, offering valuable insights for those seeking to manage emotions and behaviors through rational thought. CBT, a widely respected psychological treatment, focuses on identifying and changing negative thought patterns. Its roots can be traced back to Stoic principles, particularly the teachings of Epictetus and Marcus Aurelius. These ancient philosophers emphasized the importance of rational thinking in achieving emotional well-being, a cornerstone of CBT.

The historical development of CBT is a testament to the enduring relevance of Stoic philosophy. In the mid-20th century, psychologists like Albert Ellis and Aaron Beck pioneered CBT, drawing inspiration from Stoic ideas. As the founder of rational emotive behavior therapy (REBT), Ellis explicitly acknowledged the influence of Stoic philosophy on his work. He believed irrational beliefs and negative thinking patterns were the root causes of emotional distress, a view shared by the Stoics. Beck, the father of cognitive therapy, also incorporated Stoic principles into his approach, emphasizing the importance of challenging and reframing negative thoughts.

Both Stoicism and CBT focus on rational thought to manage emotions and behaviors. They teach that our interpretations of events, rather than the events themselves, determine our emotional responses. This shared emphasis on rational thinking is evident in techniques like cognitive restructuring, a core component of CBT. Cognitive restructuring involves identifying irrational beliefs, challenging them, and finally replacing them with more rational and balanced thoughts. This process mirrors the Stoic practice of examining and correcting false judgments, as described by Epictetus in his *Discourses*.

A common CBT technique called "thought records" illustrates the practical application of these principles. Thought records help individuals track their thoughts, identify cognitive distortions, and reframe them. For example, if you think *I always fail at everything*, a thought record would guide you to challenge this belief by examining the evidence. You might realize that while you have encountered failures, you also have many successes. This rational re-evaluation aligns with the Stoic practice of questioning and reframing negative thoughts.

Practical Exercises Combining Stoic and CBT Techniques

To help you integrate Stoic and CBT principles into your daily life, let's explore some practical exercises. Start with cognitive reframing exercises. When you encounter a distressing thought, pause and ask yourself if it is rational. Use a thought record to document the thought, challenge its validity, and reframe it. For instance, if you think, *I'm not good enough*, challenge this by listing your achievements and positive qualities. This exercise encourages a balanced perspective and reduces emotional distress.

Another effective exercise is the use of real-life scenarios. Imagine you are preparing for a job interview and feel anxious. Instead of succumbing to the anxiety, apply Stoic and CBT techniques. Identify the irrational belief driving your anxiety, such as, *If I don't get this job, I'm a failure*. Challenge this belief by considering other opportunities and reminding yourself of past successes. This rational approach helps manage anxiety and improves performance.

Case studies further demonstrate the effectiveness of integrating Stoic and CBT practices. Take, for example, a therapy session involving a client struggling with social anxiety. By combining CBT techniques with Stoic principles, a therapist can help clients identify and challenge irrational beliefs about social interactions. The client learns to reframe negative thoughts like *Everyone will judge me*, to more balanced ones like *Some people might judge me, but many others won't.* This shift in perspective reduces anxiety and enhances social confidence.

Therapists and practitioners often share success stories highlighting the transformative power of these combined approaches. One practitioner recounted a client who, through CBT and Stoic techniques, overcame a debilitating fear of public speaking. The client gradually built confidence and delivered successful speeches by challenging irrational beliefs and practicing rational reframing. Testimonials like this underscore the practical benefits of integrating Stoic wisdom with modern therapeutic techniques.

Understanding the synergy between Stoicism and CBT provides a robust framework for improving emotional resilience and mental well-being. Both approaches emphasize the importance of rational thought in managing emotions and behaviors. We can harness the wisdom of ancient philosophy and modern psychology through practical exercises and real-life applications to lead more balanced and fulfilling lives.

As we conclude this exploration, remember that the principles and techniques discussed here are not just theoretical. They are practical tools to integrate into your daily life, offering a pathway to greater emotional resilience and inner peace. The fusion of Stoic philosophy and CBT provides a rich, evidence-based approach to personal growth and well-being.

2

BUILDING EMOTIONAL RESILIENCE

Years ago, during a particularly challenging period in my career, I found myself overwhelmed by stress and anxiety. One evening, after a particularly difficult day, I recalled a technique I had read about in a book on cognitive behavioral therapy (CBT). It involved reframing my thoughts to alter my emotional responses. I decided to give it a try. To my surprise, this simple shift in perspective brought immediate relief and clarity. It was a revelation that led me to delve deeper into the practice of cognitive reframing, a method deeply rooted in Stoic philosophy, as we discussed in the previous chapter. This chapter will explore how changing your perspective can fundamentally alter your emotional landscape, providing you with tools to build mental toughness and resilience.

PREMEDITATIO MALORUM: PREPARING FOR ADVERSITY

The ancient Stoics had a unique way of preparing for life's inevitable challenges. One of their essential practices was *premeditatio malorum*, which translates to the "premeditation of evils." This Stoic exercise involves contemplating potential misfortunes before they occur. By doing so, you mentally prepare yourself for adversity, reducing the shock and emotional turmoil when those events happen. Seneca frequently practiced this technique. He once wrote, "He robs present ills of their power who has perceived their coming beforehand." Marcus Aurelius echoed this sentiment, advising, "Begin each day by telling yourself: Today I shall be meeting with interference, ingratitude, insolence, disloyalty, ill-will, and selfishness." These reflections are not meant to foster pessimism but to build resilience and mental toughness.

The psychological benefits of *premeditatio malorum* are well documented. By preparing for adversity, you increase your mental preparedness. When you expect challenges, you can develop strategies to cope effectively. This foresight reduces the impact of unexpected events. Instead of being blindsided by difficulties, you face them with a calm, composed mindset. This practice also diminishes fear and anxiety. When you envision worst-case scenarios, you realize that you can survive them. This realization fosters a sense of empowerment and reduces the fear of the unknown. As you become more accustomed to the idea of potential setbacks, you build a mental buffer against stress and anxiety.

To incorporate *premeditatio malorum* into your life, start with visualization exercises. Take a few minutes each day to imagine potential challenges you might face. For example, consider a scenario where you have to have a difficult conversation with a colleague. Visualize how the conversation might unfold, the possible objections or conflicts, and how you would calmly and effectively address them. This mental rehearsal prepares you for the event, making you more confident and composed when the time comes.

Let's look at another specific example. Imagine you are about to have a challenging performance review at work. Instead of dreading the meeting, practice *premeditatio malorum*. Visualize the possible criticisms your manager might offer. Think about how you would respond constructively, focusing on your strengths and the steps you plan to take for improvement. Preparing for this scenario reduces anxiety and increases your chances of having a productive conversation.

Reflective journaling is another powerful tool. Write about potential adversities and how you would handle them. For instance, if you are worried about a financial setback, describe the steps to manage your finances, seek additional income sources, and cut unnecessary expenses. This exercise not only prepares you mentally but also provides practical solutions. This preparation empowers you to face financial challenges with a clear and calm mind.

By mentally preparing for these scenarios, you reduce the emotional impact and increase your ability to handle them effectively. Incorporating *premeditatio malorum* into your daily routine will build resilience and mental toughness. By regularly contemplating potential adversities, you become better equipped to face life's challenges with a calm and composed mindset. This practice, deeply rooted in Stoic philosophy, offers a powerful way to reduce fear and anxiety while enhancing your ability to navigate life's inevitable ups and downs.

COGNITIVE REFRAMING: CHANGING YOUR PERSPECTIVE

Cognitive reframing is the process of changing the way you view a situation to alter its emotional impact. At its core, it involves recognizing and challenging negative thought patterns. Then, you replace them with more constructive alternatives. This practice is not about denying reality but seeing it from a different angle. The Stoics, particularly Epictetus, emphasized the power of perspective. He famously said, "It is not the things themselves that disturb people, but their judgments about these things." This quote encapsulates the essence of cognitive reframing. By changing our judgments, we change our emotional responses.

The importance of cognitive reframing in Stoic teachings cannot be overstated. Stoicism teaches that our attitudes and biases color our interpretations of events. These interpretations, rather than the events themselves, determine our emotional responses. For example, if you view a job loss as a catastrophic failure, you will likely feel despair and anxiety. However, if you see it as an opportunity for growth and new beginnings, your emotional response will be more positive. Cognitive reframing requires mindfulness and a willingness to question our automatic thoughts. Doing so can transform our emotional experiences and build greater resilience.

The benefits of cognitive reframing are numerous. First and most importantly, it reduces stress and anxiety. When we change our perspective on stressful situations, we can approach them with a calmer, more rational mindset. This shift not only alleviates immediate stress but also builds long-term emotional resilience. Improved emotional regulation is another significant benefit. By reframing negative thoughts, we gain better control over our emotional responses, leading to more balanced and stable moods. This mental toughness is crucial for navigating life's challenges, allowing us to respond to adversity with composure and clarity.

To begin practicing cognitive reframing, start by identifying negative thought patterns. Pay attention to moments when you feel stressed or anxious and note the thoughts that accompany these emotions. After you have identified these negative thoughts, challenge them with evidence and logic. Question if your thoughts are based on assumptions or facts. For example, if you think *I'll never be successful*, question the validity of this statement. Find evidence of past successes and remind yourself of your skills and qualities.

Replace the negative thought with a more balanced and constructive one, such as, *I've faced challenges before and succeeded; I can do it again.*

Let's consider a real-life example. Imagine a professional who feels overwhelmed by workplace stress. They might think, *I can't handle this workload; I will fail.* By practicing cognitive reframing, they can challenge this thought by recalling times when they successfully managed heavy workloads. They might reframe their thought to, *This is a challenging situation, but I've handled similar ones before and succeeded. I can break this task into manageable steps.* This new perspective reduces anxiety and fosters a sense of competence and control.

Exercise: Journaling Negative Thoughts and Writing Positive Alternatives

A practical exercise to reinforce cognitive reframing is journaling. Start by writing down a negative thought you frequently experience. Next, challenge this thought with evidence. Finally, write a more positive and balanced alternative. For instance, if you often think, *I'm not good enough,* challenge this by listing your achievements and positive qualities. Then replace the thought with, *I have many skills and accomplishments that prove my worth.* Regularly practicing this exercise will help you internalize the habit of cognitive reframing, leading to improved emotional resilience and mental toughness.

Integrating cognitive reframing into your daily life can change how you react to stress and adversity. This practice, deeply rooted in Stoic philosophy, empowers you to take control of your emotional responses and build lasting resilience. It is a powerful tool that, when consistently applied, can lead to profound changes in your mental and emotional well-being.

THE ART OF SELF-DISCIPLINE: STAYING FOCUSED AND COMMITTED

Self-discipline is a core tenet of Stoic philosophy, crucial for building resilience and achieving personal excellence. Within the Stoic framework, self-discipline involves controlling one's impulses, focusing on long-term goals, and acting according to rational principles. The Stoics viewed self-discipline as a critical component of virtue, fundamental to living a life of moral integrity and inner strength. In *Meditations*, Marcus Aurelius often reflected on the importance of self-discipline, noting that true freedom comes from mastery over oneself. By cultivating self-discipline, you strengthen your resolve and enhance your capacity to face life's challenges with composure and determination.

Cultivating self-discipline requires actionable strategies that you can incorporate into your daily routine. One effective technique is to set clear goals and priorities. Start by determining what is very important to you in the short and long term. Write your goals down and break them down into manageable steps. Clarifying your goals and steps will help you stay motivated and focused and give a roadmap for your actions.

Additionally, creating and adhering to routines is essential for developing self-discipline. Establish a schedule each day for work, exercise, and relaxation. Consistency is key. By following a structured routine, you build habits that support your goals and reduce the likelihood of procrastination.

Practical exercises can further enhance your self-discipline. Start your day with a morning routine that sets the tone for focus and productivity. This might include activities like a brief workout, meditation, or journaling. These practices help center your mind and prepare you for the day's tasks. Another valuable technique for overcoming procrastination is the "two-minute rule." Do a task immediately if it only takes you less than two minutes. This simple rule helps you tackle small tasks efficiently, preventing them from piling up and overwhelming you. For more significant tasks, break them down into manageable, small steps with specific deadlines for each one.

Consider a marathon runner preparing for a race who exemplifies the power of self-discipline. Training for a marathon requires unwavering commitment and rigorous preparation. This runner starts the day with a disciplined routine, including early morning runs, balanced nutrition, and adequate rest. Adhering to this regimen builds the physical and mental endurance needed to complete the marathon successfully. Similarly, a disciplined approach can lead to significant career growth in the professional realm. Take the example of a professional who sets clear career goals and consistently works toward them. They dedicate themselves daily to skill development, networking, and seeking new opportunities. Over time, this disciplined approach results in promotions, new job offers, and personal fulfillment.

Self-discipline also plays a crucial role in maintaining balance and avoiding burnout. By setting boundaries and prioritizing self-care, you ensure that your pursuit of goals does not come at the expense of your well-being. For instance, incorporating regular breaks and leisure activities into your schedule helps recharge your energy and maintain focus. This balance is vital to sustain productivity long-term and reach your goals without compromising your health.

The Stoic practice of voluntary hardship is another powerful technique for building self-discipline. This involves deliberately subjecting yourself to minor difficulties to strengthen your resilience. For example, taking cold showers, fasting, or engaging in challenging physical activities can help you build mental toughness.

By willingly facing discomfort, you train your mind to remain steadfast in adversity. This practice enhances your self-discipline and prepares you for unexpected challenges.

Incorporating these exercises and strategies into daily life can significantly enhance self-discipline. By setting clear goals, creating routines, and practicing voluntary hardship, you build the mental toughness and resilience needed to achieve your aspirations. The stories of successful individuals, from marathon runners to career professionals, illustrate the transformative power of self-discipline. As you cultivate this virtue, you will be better equipped to navigate life's challenges with focus, commitment, and unwavering determination.

MANAGING ANGER: STOIC STRATEGIES FOR EMOTIONAL CONTROL

The emotion of anger can quickly take over, leading to regrettable consequences. Stoic principles provide practical strategies for managing and dissipating anger, turning it from a destructive force into a manageable emotion. According to Stoicism, anger is a natural reaction that should be controlled through rational thought and self-awareness. Seneca offers extensive advice on anger management. He wrote, "The greatest remedy for anger is delay." This simple yet profound idea underscores the importance of taking a moment to pause and reflect before reacting in anger.

Uncontrolled anger can have significant negative impacts on various aspects of life. In personal relationships, anger can create rifts, breed resentment, and lead to misunderstandings. A single outburst can damage trust and intimacy, making it difficult to repair the relationship. The effects extend to physical and mental health as well. Chronic anger may increase stress levels, cause high blood pressure, and weaken the immune system. Concerning mental health, it can contribute to anxiety, depression, and a sense of constant agitation. These repercussions highlight why managing anger effectively and maintaining emotional balance is crucial.

Practical techniques for managing anger are essential for incorporating Stoic principles into daily life. One effective method is deep breathing exercises. If you begin to feel angry, take slow, deep breaths to calm your nervous system. Inhale deeply through your nose. Hold your breath for a few seconds. Then, exhale slowly through your mouth. This physiological response can help reduce the intensity of your anger, giving you time to think before you act. Another technique is cognitive reframing, which involves changing how you interpret and respond to anger-inducing situations. Ask yourself if the source of your anger is essential in the grand scheme. Often, the answer is no, and this realization can help diffuse your anger.

Reflecting on past instances of anger can also be a powerful tool for managing future outbursts. Take some time to think about a recent situation where you felt angry. What triggered your anger? How did you respond? What were the consequences? Consider alternative responses that could have led to a more positive outcome. This reflection helps you understand your triggers and develop strategies for responding more calmly in the future. For example, if you often get angry during heated work meetings, think about how you could handle these situations differently. You could take a moment to breathe deeply, remind yourself to stay calm and respond with a composed and measured tone.

Let's consider a real-life scenario. Imagine you are in a heated argument at work, and a colleague makes a comment that makes you mad. Instead of reacting impulsively, take a deep breath and count to ten. This brief pause allows you to calm down and think more clearly. Ask yourself if the comment is worth getting angry over. Is it possible that your colleague didn't mean to offend you? By reframing your perspective, you can respond in a constructive way instead of an aggressive way. This approach helps you manage your anger and sets a positive example for others.

Exercise: Reflecting on Past Instances of Anger and Alternative Responses

To reinforce these techniques, try an exercise in reflection. Consider a recent instance where you felt angry and write about it in detail. What triggered your anger? How did you respond? What were the consequences? Next, brainstorm alternative responses that could have yielded a more positive outcome. Write these down as well. This exercise helps you gain insight into triggers and brainstorm strategies for managing your anger more effectively in the future.

By incorporating these Stoic strategies for managing anger, you can transform this powerful emotion into a tool for growth and self-improvement. The principles of deep breathing, cognitive reframing, and reflective exercises provide practical and effective ways to maintain emotional control and improve your overall well-being. When managed well, anger can become a catalyst for positive change rather than a source of regret and harm.

OVERCOMING ANXIETY: STOIC TECHNIQUES FOR CALMNESS

Anxiety can be a persistent and overwhelming emotion, but Stoic philosophy offers practical techniques to help calm the mind. Stoics understood that anxiety often stems from our perceptions and judgments about events rather than the events themselves. Epictetus famously said, "Men are disturbed not by things, but by the views which they take of them." This insight lies at the heart of the Stoic approach to overcoming anxiety. By changing how we view and respond to situations, we can reduce our anxiety and regain a sense of calm.

The Stoic approach to managing anxiety involves several practices designed to improve mental clarity and enhance emotional stability. One of the primary benefits of Stoic techniques is the development of a calmer mind. We can think more clearly and make better decisions when we learn to see things as they are without attaching unnecessary judgments or fears. This mental clarity is crucial for navigating stressful situations effectively. Additionally, Stoic practices help stabilize our emotions. By focusing on what we can control and accepting what we cannot, we create a more balanced and resilient emotional state. This stability allows us to face challenges with confidence and composure.

To manage anxiety effectively, consider incorporating mindfulness and meditation practices into your daily routine. Mindfulness is paying attention to the present moment without judgment. Focusing on the here and now can quiet the mind and reduce anxious thoughts about the future. Meditation, primarily guided Stoic meditation, can help cultivate this mindfulness. Start with a few minutes each day. Sit quietly and focus on your breath. Breathe in and out and observe your thoughts without getting caught up in them. This simple practice can help create a headspace where anxiety can dissipate.

Another powerful technique for reducing anxiety is cognitive reframing. When you notice anxious thoughts, challenge them with evidence and logic. Determine if your thoughts are based on facts or assumptions. For example, if you are worried about an upcoming presentation, you might think, *I will fail, and everyone will judge me.* Challenge this thought by recalling past successes and reminding yourself of your preparation. Reframe thinking to something more balanced, such as, *I have prepared well, and I can handle this presentation.* This perspective shift can significantly reduce anxiety.

Exercise: Daily Mindfulness Meditation

To practice mindfulness meditation, do the following:

1. Pick a quiet space to sit comfortably.
2. Close your eyes and take some deep breaths.
3. Focus attention on your breath as it flows in and out.
4. Gently bring focus back to your breathing if your mind wanders.

Do this practice for five to ten minutes each day. Over time, this meditation will help calm your mind and reduce anxiety.

Let's consider a specific scenario where Stoic principles can help manage anxiety. Imagine you have an important presentation at work and feel anxious about it. Instead of succumbing to the stress, apply Stoic techniques. Begin with a few minutes of mindfulness meditation to calm your mind. Then, use cognitive reframing to challenge any negative thoughts. Remind yourself of your preparation and past successes. Visualize yourself delivering the presentation confidently and effectively. Combining mindfulness and cognitive reframing helps reduce anxiety and enhances your performance.

Integrating these Stoic techniques into your daily life can overcome anxiety and cultivate a sense of calmness. Mindfulness, meditation, and cognitive reframing provide practical and effective ways to manage anxious thoughts and emotions. These practices, rooted in ancient Stoic wisdom, offer powerful ways to navigate the complexities of modern life with greater ease and confidence.

DEALING WITH JEALOUSY: CULTIVATING CONTENTMENT

Jealousy, a familiar yet corrosive emotion, often stems from comparing ourselves to others. According to Stoic philosophy, jealousy is seen as a misjudgment of values. The Stoics believed true contentment comes from within, not external achievements or possessions. Marcus Aurelius advises us in *Meditations*, "The happiness of your life depends upon the quality of your thoughts." This underscores the Stoic view that jealousy is a result of misplaced focus. We can cultivate genuine contentment by shifting our attention from what others have to our inner virtues and achievements.

The adverse effects of jealousy are profound and far-reaching. In relationships, jealousy can breed resentment and mistrust, eroding the foundation of love and companionship. It can lead to low self-esteem and feeling inadequate as we constantly measure ourselves against others. This mental and emotional drain detracts us from appreciating our lives and achievements. The energy expended on jealousy could be better used for personal growth and self-improvement. Recognizing these detrimental effects is the first step toward overcoming jealousy and fostering emotional well-being.

Practical techniques rooted in Stoic philosophy can effectively overcome jealousy and cultivate contentment. One such technique is practicing gratitude. By focusing on what we already have and appreciating the positives in our lives, we shift our attention away from what we lack. Begin a daily gratitude journal by listing three things you are grateful for daily. This simple practice can change your mindset and help you see the abundance in your life. Reflecting on your achievements is another powerful tool. Take time to acknowledge your accomplishments, no matter how small. This reflection builds self-esteem and reduces the tendency to compare yourself to others.

Consider the story of a professional who struggled with workplace jealousy. This individual constantly compared their career progress to their colleagues, leading to feelings of inadequacy and frustration. Through self-reflection and practicing gratitude, they began to shift their focus. They started a gratitude journal and regularly reflected on their achievements. Over time, they noticed a significant change in their mindset. Instead of feeling envious of their colleagues, they felt content and proud of their progress. This shift improved their emotional well-being and enhanced their professional relationships.

Exercise: Daily Gratitude Journaling

To reinforce the practice of gratitude, try a daily gratitude journaling exercise. Each evening, write down three things you are grateful for. These can be as simple as a good meal, a kind word from a friend, or a personal achievement. Over time, you will find that this practice helps you focus on the positives in your life and reduces feelings of jealousy.

Practicing gratitude and reflecting on your achievements are potent ways to shift your focus from what others have to what you possess. Integrating these Stoic techniques into your daily routine can transform jealousy into contentment. This change in perspective fosters a sense of inner peace and satisfaction, allowing you to appreciate your life fully.

Recognizing the detrimental effects of jealousy and employing these practical strategies will help you build emotional resilience and contentment. As you continue to explore Stoic principles, you will find that these practices enhance your overall quality of life and improve your emotional well-being.

In this chapter, we have explored several Stoic techniques for building emotional resilience. From cognitive reframing to managing jealousy, these strategies provide practical tools for navigating life's challenges with more stability and peace. As we move forward, we will delve into daily practices that further solidify these concepts, helping you cultivate a Stoic mindset in every aspect of your life.

3

INNER PEACE THROUGH MEDITATION AND REFLECTION

Quite a few years ago, I struggled with daily life's chaos. One morning, I decided to try something different. Instead of jumping out of bed and diving into my hectic routine, I woke up early, found a quiet spot, and spent ten minutes meditating. This simple practice set the tone for the rest of my day. I felt more centered, focused, and ready to tackle whatever came my way. It was my first encounter with the transformative power of morning meditation, a practice deeply rooted in Stoic philosophy.

MORNING MEDITATION: SETTING INTENTIONS FOR THE DAY

Starting your day with morning meditation is like laying a solid foundation for a building. It aligns your mind with Stoic principles, setting a positive tone to influence your daily actions and decisions. Marcus Aurelius understood this well. He wrote extensively about his morning routines in his journal (*Meditations*). By beginning his day with reflection and intention-setting, Aurelius cultivated mental clarity and resilience, which guided him in personal and imperial matters.

The benefits of morning meditation are numerous. First, it enhances mental clarity. When you start your day with a calm and focused mind, you can approach tasks with greater concentration and efficiency. Morning meditation also reduces stress and anxiety, providing inner peace that carries you through the day's challenges. Moreover, it fosters a positive mindset, helping you respond to situations with composure and wisdom. This practice aligns with the Stoic belief in the power of rational thought and self-control. We will combine several ideas covered in the first two chapters to create a beneficial morning routine of meditation and intentions.

We reviewed a basic mindfulness routine in the previous chapter, but it is worth revisiting. To incorporate morning meditation into your routine, settle into a quiet space where you will not be bothered. Sit in a comfortable position, whether it is on a chair, cushion, or directly on the floor. Close your eyes and take a few deep breaths to center yourself. Focus on your breath, feeling the sensation of each inhale and exhale. Acknowledge that thoughts arise without judgment and gently bring your focus back to your breath. This simple breathing helps anchor your mind in the present moment, setting a calm and focused tone for the day ahead.

Once you are centered, set your intentions for the day. These intentions should align with the Stoic principles discussed in Chapter 1, focusing on virtue and character. Consider what kind of person you want to be and what values you want to embody. For example, you set the intention to practice patience, show kindness, or remain resilient in facing challenges. Setting intentions for personal growth and resilience helps you navigate your day purposefully and clearly. It provides a moral compass to direct decisions and actions so they align with your highest values.

In addition to setting intentions, you can enhance your morning meditation with visualization techniques. Visualize yourself moving through your day with grace and virtue. Picture how you will handle various situations, from mundane tasks to potential challenges, with composure and wisdom. This mental rehearsal prepares you for the day and reinforces your commitment to Stoic principles. Visualization helps you embody the virtues you aspire to, making them a natural part of your daily interactions. (We will review negative visualization a bit later in this chapter.)

Breathing exercises are another valuable component of morning meditation. Start with a simple practice like diaphragmatic breathing. It is when you breathe deeply into your belly rather than shallowly into your chest. This breathing practice activates the body's relaxation response, reducing stress and calming you. Alternatively, try the 4-7-8 technique:

1. Inhale for four counts.
2. Hold your breath for seven counts.
3. Exhale for eight counts.

This exercise can help center your mind and body, enhancing the overall effectiveness of your meditation. Integrating morning meditation into your daily routine sets a positive and intentional tone.

This practice, rooted in Stoic philosophy, offers numerous benefits, from enhanced mental clarity to reduced stress. It helps you align your actions with your values, fostering personal growth and resilience. Whether through visualization, breathing exercises, or simply setting intentions, morning meditation provides a powerful tool for cultivating inner peace and living a life guided by virtue.

GUIDED STOIC MEDITATIONS: AUDIO AND VIDEO RESOURCES

Guided meditations enhance the meditation experience by providing structure and support, especially for those new to the practice. Audio and video resources can make this process effective and even more accessible. Modern Stoic practitioners often emphasize the benefits of guided meditations, highlighting how these tools can help maintain focus and deepen the meditative state. For instance, listening to a soothing voice guide you through meditation can reduce distractions and help you stay present. Video resources add a visual element, which can be particularly helpful for guided visualizations and breathing exercises.

Several types of guided Stoic meditations align with Stoic principles. Breathing exercises for mindfulness are a common technique. These exercises involve focusing on your breath to anchor your mind in the present moment. A guided session might prompt you to pay attention to your breath entering and leaving your body, helping you cultivate mindfulness. Another valuable technique is guided visualization for resilience. This involves imagining yourself facing and overcoming challenges, reinforcing your mental strength and preparedness. For example, a guided meditation might take you through a scenario where you handle a difficult conversation calmly and with composure, helping you internalize these qualities.

Numerous audio and video resources are available to help you get started with guided Stoic meditations. Apps like Calm and Headspace offer a variety of guided meditation sessions that can be easily integrated into your daily routine. Websites such as Daily Stoic provide specific Stoic-themed meditations, often accompanied by reflections from ancient Stoic texts. YouTube is another excellent resource, with channels dedicated to Stoic philosophy offering guided meditations and visualizations. For instance, you might find a session focused on practicing gratitude or building resilience, each designed to align with Stoic principles.

Integrating guided meditations into your daily routine requires consistency and a conducive environment. Set a regular meditation schedule that fits your lifestyle. It could be first thing in the morning, during a lunch break, or before bed. The key is to make it a habit. Create a space that is quiet and free from distractions. It might be a corner in your bedroom, living room, or peaceful outdoor spot. Ensure that this space is comfortable and inviting, with minimal interruptions. Over time, this designated meditation space will become a sanctuary for your practice, helping you maintain consistency and focus.

Using guided meditations can also help you explore different techniques and find what resonates with you. For instance, you might start with a simple breathing exercise to calm your mind and then move on to a guided visualization for resilience. Experiment with different sessions and notice how they impact your mental and emotional state. Jot down your experiences in a journal, noting which techniques are most effective for you. This detailed approach ensures that your meditation practice remains dynamic and aligned with your evolving needs.

Incorporating guided Stoic meditations into your daily life can enhance your emotional resilience, mental clarity, and overall well-being. The structure provided by audio and video resources makes it easier to maintain focus and deepen your practice. If you are a beginner or an experienced meditator, these tools offer valuable support on your path to inner peace and personal growth. The variety of techniques available, from mindfulness breathing exercises to guided visualizations, lets you tailor your practice to your specific needs and goals. The key is to be consistent, create a conducive environment, and remain open to exploring different approaches.

VISUALIZATION TECHNIQUES: PRACTICING NEGATIVE VISUALIZATION

Negative visualization is a powerful Stoic practice that involves contemplating potential misfortunes to build resilience and appreciation for what you have. This technique, known as *premeditatio malorum* in Latin, was widely practiced by ancient Stoic philosophers like Seneca, who famously advised, "Set aside a certain number of days, during which you shall be content with the scantiest and cheapest fare, with coarse and rough dress, saying to yourself the while: 'Is this the condition that I feared?'" By imagining the worst-case scenarios, you mentally prepare yourself for adversity, making you less reactive and more grateful for your current circumstances.

The psychological benefits of negative visualization are substantial. First, it increases mental preparedness. When you regularly contemplate potential challenges, you become more adept at handling them when they arise. This mental rehearsal reduces the shock and stress associated with unexpected events. For example, if you imagine losing your job, you can plan how to manage your finances and seek new opportunities, making you more resilient if such a situation occurs.

Additionally, negative visualization fosters greater appreciation for your current circumstances. By contemplating the loss of things you often take for granted, you develop a more profound gratitude for them. This shift in perspective enhances your overall well-being and contentment.

To practice negative visualization effectively, find a quiet space to focus without distractions. Sit comfortably and close your eyes. Begin by taking a few deep breaths to center your mind. Once you are calm, visualize a specific challenge or misfortune. Imagine it in vivid detail, considering how it would impact your life. For instance, imagine a day without modern conveniences like electricity or running water. Picture yourself navigating this scenario and reflect on how you would cope. This exercise helps you appreciate the conveniences you currently enjoy and prepares you mentally for potential disruptions.

Visualizing potential obstacles in your personal and professional life can also be highly beneficial. Imagine facing a significant setback at work, such as a failed project or a missed promotion. Visualize how you would handle the disappointment and what steps you would take to move forward. This mental rehearsal equips you with strategies to manage real-life challenges, reducing anxiety and increasing resilience. Similarly, contemplate potential obstacles in your personal life, such as relationship conflicts or health issues. By preparing mentally for these scenarios, you become more capable of handling them with composure and wisdom.

Practical Application: Visualizing a Day Without Modern Conveniences

To make negative visualization a regular practice, schedule sessions once or twice a week. During these sessions, spend 5-10 minutes contemplating specific challenges. Start with simple scenarios, like imagining a day without modern conveniences. Picture yourself waking up without electricity, running water, or internet access. Think about how you would adapt to this situation. What alternative solutions would you find? How would you manage your daily tasks? This exercise helps you appreciate the conveniences you often take for granted and prepares you for potential disruptions.

Another practical application is to visualize potential obstacles in your personal and professional life. For instance, imagine facing a major financial setback. Visualize losing a significant portion of your income and consider how you would manage your finances. Think about the steps you would take to cut expenses, find additional income sources, and maintain your financial stability. This mental rehearsal prepares you for potential financial challenges and reduces the anxiety associated with uncertainty.

Incorporating negative visualization into your routine builds mental resilience and fosters a deeper appreciation for your current circumstances. This Stoic practice helps you navigate life's challenges with greater ease and composure, turning potential misfortunes into opportunities for growth and gratitude.

THE DISCIPLINE OF JOURNALING: DAILY STOIC PRACTICE

Journaling has long been a cornerstone of Stoic practice, a powerful tool for self-awareness and personal growth. By putting pen to paper, you can internalize Stoic teachings and reflect on your daily actions, thoughts, and emotions. This fosters a deeper understanding of your behaviors and helps you align them with Stoic principles. The benefits of daily journaling are numerous. It lets you track your progress, identify areas to improve, and cultivate a mindset of continuous growth. Moreover, journaling provides a safe space to explore your innermost thoughts and feelings, promoting emotional resilience and mental clarity.

Historically, Stoic philosophers like Marcus Aurelius and Seneca were avid journal keepers. Marcus Aurelius's *Meditations* is a prime example of Stoic journaling. In his writings, he reflected on his daily experiences, examined his thoughts, and reinforced his commitment to Stoic virtues. Seneca, too, used journaling as a means of self-examination, often writing letters to himself to explore philosophical ideas and moral dilemmas. These historical examples highlight the enduring value of journaling in Stoic practice. By following in their footsteps, you can harness the transformative power of reflective writing.

Setting aside dedicated time each day is crucial to maintain a consistent journaling practice. Choose a time that works best for you, whether in the morning, during lunch, or before bed. Consistency is vital, as regular journaling helps reinforce the habit and deepen its impact. Using prompts can also guide your journaling sessions and ensure they remain focused and purposeful. Prompts can range from questions about your daily actions and decisions to reflections on your emotions and thoughts. These prompts serve as a starting point, helping you delve deeper into your experiences and extract valuable insights.

There are various types of Stoic journaling that you can explore. Reflective journaling involves examining your daily actions and behaviors through the lens of Stoic principles. This type of journaling encourages you to assess how well your actions align with your values and identify areas for improvement. For example, you might reflect on a challenging interaction with a colleague and consider how you could have responded with more patience and understanding. On the other hand, gratitude journaling focuses on cultivating contentment by acknowledging the positives in your life. By regularly listing things you are grateful for, you shift your focus from what you lack to what you have, fostering a sense of inner peace and satisfaction.

To get started with your journaling practice, here are some practical prompts. Reflect on the four cardinal virtues—Wisdom, Justice,

Courage, and Moderation—and consider how they manifested in your actions today. Ask yourself questions like, "Did I act with wisdom in my decisions?" and "How did I practice justice in my interactions?" These prompts help you evaluate your day through the lens of Stoic virtues, reinforcing your commitment to ethical living. Another useful exercise is to reflect on daily challenges and learning experiences. Write about a specific challenge you faced and what you learned from it. Consider how to apply these lessons in the future to navigate similar situations with greater ease and wisdom.

Exercise: Reflecting on Daily Challenges and Learning Experiences

To reinforce your reflective journaling practice, try this exercise. At the end of each day, take a few minutes to write about a challenge you encountered. Describe the experience in detail and reflect on your response. What did you learn from this situation? Moving forward, how can you apply this lesson? This exercise helps you gain valuable insights from your daily experiences, fostering continuous growth and self-improvement.

Incorporating these journaling techniques into your daily routine can deepen your understanding of Stoic principles and enhance your personal growth. Reflective writing and gratitude journaling offer powerful tools for self-examination and contentment, helping you navigate life's complexities with greater clarity and resilience. The prompts and exercises serve as a starting point, guiding you toward continuous self-discovery and improvement.

Reflective Questions: Engaging with Stoic Wisdom

Reflective questions are a potent tool for deepening your understanding of Stoic philosophy and internalizing its teachings. By asking yourself thought-provoking questions, you can explore your actions, thoughts, and emotions, gaining insights that promote self-awareness and personal growth. The Stoics, including great philosophers like Epictetus and Seneca, often used reflective questioning to examine their lives and align their behavior with their values. This practice encourages you to engage actively with Stoic principles, making them a tangible part of your daily life rather than abstract concepts.

Engaging with reflective questions offers numerous benefits. One of the most significant is enhanced self-reflection. By regularly examining your actions and thoughts, you become more aware of your strengths and areas for improvement. This self-awareness is vital for personal growth, because it enables you to make conscious decisions that align with your values and goals. Moreover, reflective questioning improves decision-making. When you take the time to reflect on past decisions and their outcomes, you gain valuable insights that inform your future choices. This practice promotes emotional regulation by helping you understand your emotions' underlying causes, enabling you to manage them more effectively.

To help you incorporate reflective questioning into your routine, consider the following curated list of questions that align with Stoic principles. These questions guide your self-examination and foster a deeper understanding of your actions and emotions. Ask yourself about daily actions and decisions: "Did I act following my values today?" "How did I respond to challenges?" and "What could I have done differently?" These questions help you assess how well your actions align with Stoic virtues and identify areas for improvement. For personal growth and virtue cultivation, consider questions like: "What virtues did I embody today?" "How did I practice wisdom, justice, courage, and moderation?" and "What steps can I take to cultivate these virtues further?"

Reflective questions can be incorporated into your daily life through simple yet effective exercises. One practical way is to set aside time each evening for reflection. Find a quiet, comfortable spot to review your day. Then, use the provided questions to guide your reflection and write down your thoughts and insights. This practice reinforces your commitment to Stoic principles and helps you internalize the lessons learned. Another practical approach is to use reflective questions in your journaling sessions. As you write about your experiences, incorporate the questions to prompt deeper exploration and understanding. This combination of writing and reflection enhances the impact of both practices, fostering continuous growth and self-awareness.

Exercise: Setting Aside Time Each Evening for Reflection

Dedicate a few minutes each evening to this exercise to make reflective questioning a regular practice. Sit quietly and review your day, using the reflective questions to guide your thoughts. Write down your insights and observations. For example, consider a challenging interaction you had and ask: "How did I respond?" "What could I have done differently?" and "What did I learn from this experience?" This exercise helps you gain valuable insights from your daily experiences, promoting continuous improvement and alignment with Stoic principles.

Engaging with reflective questions can deepen your understanding of Stoic philosophy and enhance your personal growth. This practice promotes self-awareness, improves decision-making, and fosters emotional regulation. The curated list of questions is a starting point, guiding you toward continuous self-discovery and improvement. By asking these questions daily, you make Stoic principles a tangible part of your life, fostering a constant growth mindset and alignment with your values.

Evening Reflection: Reviewing Your Actions

As the day winds down, a moment of reflection can offer profound insights into your actions and thoughts. Evening reflection, a practice deeply embedded in Stoic philosophy, provides a structured way to review your day, fostering personal growth and self-awareness. The Stoics, including Seneca and Marcus Aurelius, emphasized the importance of this practice. Marcus Aurelius, in *Meditations*, often reflected on his behavior and decisions, seeking to align them with his values. In his letters, Seneca advised daily self-examination to understand one's progress and areas needing improvement. This nightly introspection was not just about self-criticism but learning and evolving.

The benefits of evening reflection go beyond mere self-assessment. It promotes a deeper understanding of your actions, thoughts, and emotions to help you identify patterns and areas for growth. This practice enhances self-awareness, allowing you to recognize your strengths and weaknesses. It also fosters a sense of accountability as you take responsibility for your actions and their consequences. By consistently reflecting on your day, you cultivate a continuous improvement mindset, aligning your daily actions with your long-term goals and values.

To practice evening reflection effectively, follow a structured approach. Start by going to a quiet spot where you can sit comfortably without distractions. Reflect on your actions, thoughts, and emotions throughout the day. Consider moments of success and areas where you could have acted differently. Identify specific actions that aligned with your values and those that did not. This reflection helps you recognize positive behaviors to reinforce and negative ones to address. Write down these observations, as writing can deepen your understanding and commitment to change.

Self-compassion plays an essential role in this process. It is vital to see the difference between constructive criticism and self-judgment. Constructive criticism involves acknowledging areas for improvement without harsh self-criticism. It is about learning and growing, not punishing yourself for mistakes. Marcus Aurelius, a master of balance, wrote, "When you arise in the morning, think of what a privilege it is to be alive, to think, to enjoy, to love." This quote underscores the importance of self-compassion. Reflect on your day with kindness, recognizing that everyone makes mistakes and each day is an opportunity to learn and improve.

Incorporate specific reflection prompts to guide your evening reflection. Ask yourself, "What did I do well today?" and "What could I have done better?" Consider how your actions align with your values and identify areas for growth. Reflect on your emotional responses and how they influenced your behavior. Did you react with patience and understanding, or were there moments of frustration and anger? These questions help you better understand your behavior and its impact, paving the way for positive change.

Exercise: Writing a Nightly Summary of Challenges and Successes

To reinforce your evening reflection, try writing a nightly summary. Each evening, take a few minutes to write about the success you had and the challenges you faced. Focus on specific actions and their outcomes. Think of what you learned from these experiences and how you can apply these lessons. This exercise helps you internalize your reflections and commit to continuous improvement. Over time, you will notice patterns in your behavior and identify strategies for overcoming recurring challenges.

Integrating evening reflection into your nightly routine creates a powerful tool for self-improvement. This practice, rooted in Stoic philosophy, helps you align your actions with your values. It fosters personal growth and self-awareness. The structured approach, guided by reflection prompts and self-compassion, ensures you learn from each day and strive to improve.

In this chapter, we have explored various practices for cultivating inner peace through meditation and reflection. From morning meditation to evening reflection, journaling, and negative visualization, each technique offers unique benefits for personal growth and self-awareness. As we continue, we will dive into practical applications of Stoic principles in modern life, helping you navigate today's challenges with wisdom and resilience.

4

PRACTICAL APPLICATIONS IN MODERN LIFE

A few years ago, I found myself endlessly scrolling through social media, comparing my life to the curated highlights of others. Each swipe deepened my sense of inadequacy. It was not until I stumbled upon the teachings of Epictetus that I realized how much control I had relinquished to my screen. He said, "It is not the things themselves that disturb us, but our judgments about these things." This wisdom prompted me to reassess my relationship with social media and to apply Stoic principles to regain my mental well-being.

MODERN MINDFULNESS: INTEGRATING STOICISM INTO DAILY LIFE

Modern mindfulness and Stoicism share a deep connection, emphasizing the importance of presence and awareness in daily life. In the Stoic context, mindfulness involves a heightened awareness of one's thoughts, actions, and surroundings. Marcus Aurelius often reflected on the importance of living in the present. He wrote, "Confine yourself to the present" and "The happiness of your life depends upon the quality of your thoughts." These quotes underscore the Stoic belief that true contentment comes from focusing on the present moment and maintaining a vigilant awareness of our internal states.

Incorporating Stoic mindfulness into daily life can significantly enhance your mental well-being. One practical approach is mindful breathing. This involves focusing solely on your breath for a few moments each day. Sit in a comfortable position, close your eyes, and breathe deeply. Pay attention to the sensation of the air entering and leaving your body. This simple practice helps anchor your mind in the present, reducing stress and promoting a sense of calm. Another effective technique is reflective meditation. At the end of each day, take a few minutes to reflect on your actions and decisions. Consider how they align with your values and Stoic principles. This reflection fosters greater self-awareness and helps you make more intentional choices.

The benefits of Stoic mindfulness for mental well-being are profound. Practicing mindfulness improves focus and concentration. When you train your mind to stay present, you become more attentive and engaged in your tasks. This heightened focus leads to greater productivity and a sense of accomplishment. Mindfulness also reduces stress and anxiety. You can nurture a more balanced and peaceful mind by staying present and not getting lost in worries about the future or regrets about the past. This emotional stability is crucial for navigating life's challenges with resilience and grace.

To illustrate the practical application of Stoic mindfulness, consider the story of an individual who struggled with chronic anxiety. They decided to integrate mindful breathing and reflective meditation into their daily routine. Each morning, they spent five minutes focusing on their breath, which helped them start the day with a calm and clear mind. In the evenings, they reflected on their actions and decisions, considering how to improve. Over time, these practices significantly reduced their anxiety and improved their overall well-being. They felt more in control of their emotions and better equipped to handle stress.

Exercise: Practicing Mindful Walking and Reflecting on Sensory Experiences

A practical exercise to deepen your mindfulness practice is mindful walking. Find a quiet location where you can walk without distractions. As you walk, pay close attention to each step. Notice the rhythm of your breathing, your feet touching the ground, and the sounds and sights around you. This practice helps you stay present and fully engage with your surroundings. After your walk, take a few minutes to reflect on your sensory experiences. Write down what you noticed and how it made you feel. This exercise enhances your awareness and appreciation of the present moment.

Integrating Stoic mindfulness into your daily life allows you to grow a more profound sense of awareness and presence. Mindful breathing, reflective meditation, and mindful walking are practical techniques that help you stay grounded and focused. These practices improve mental clarity and emotional stability and foster greater inner peace. Whether you are dealing with stress, anxiety, or the demands of daily life, Stoic mindfulness offers powerful tools to enhance your well-being and live more intentionally.

BUILDING EMOTIONAL INTELLIGENCE: STOIC PRINCIPLES IN RELATIONSHIPS

Emotional intelligence is a crucial aspect of Stoic philosophy, particularly in the context of relationships. It involves recognizing, understanding, and managing our feelings and other's emotions.

Epictetus emphasized this when he said, "It's not what happens to you, but how you react to it that matters." This quote encapsulates the essence of emotional intelligence within Stoicism. Emotional intelligence includes self-awareness, self-regulation, empathy, and social skills. These elements are vital for maintaining healthy relationships and navigating social interactions with grace and wisdom.

Enhancing emotional intelligence through Stoic practices involves several actionable steps. One key strategy is practicing empathy. Empathy lets us understand and share the feelings of others. To develop empathy, try to view situations from another person's perspective. Ask yourself how they might feel and what they might be experiencing. This practice fosters deeper connections and reduces conflicts. Another critical step is reflecting on your emotional responses and triggers. Take time to identify what situations or behaviors elicit strong emotional reactions. Understanding these triggers helps you manage your responses more effectively, preventing unnecessary conflicts and misunderstandings.

Self-awareness and self-regulation are foundational to emotional intelligence. Self-awareness involves recognizing your emotions and understanding their impact on your behavior. One technique for increasing self-awareness is keeping an emotion journal. Regularly write down your feelings and reflect on the events that triggered them. This practice helps you identify patterns and gain insights into your emotional landscape. Self-regulation, on the other hand, is about controlling your emotional responses. Stoicism teaches us to pause and reflect before reacting. When faced with an emotionally charged situation, take a moment to breathe and assess your feelings. Ask yourself if your reaction aligns with your values and long-term goals. This pause allows you to respond thoughtfully rather than impulsively.

Real-life examples can illustrate the power of these practices in building emotional intelligence. Consider a couple who struggled with frequent arguments and misunderstandings. They decided to practice Stoic empathy by genuinely trying to understand each other's perspectives. Additionally, they reflected on their emotional triggers and worked on self-regulation techniques. Their relationship significantly improved over time. They communicated more effectively, resolved conflicts quickly, and felt more connected. This story demonstrates how Stoic principles can transform relationships by fostering empathy, self-awareness, and emotional control.

Exercise: Reflecting on Recent Interactions and Identifying Emotional Triggers

To apply these principles in your own life, try this exercise. Reflect on a recent interaction that elicited a strong emotional response. Write down the details of the interaction, including what was said and how you felt. Identify the specific emotions you experienced and the triggers that caused them. Consider how you reacted and whether it aligned with your values. Reflect on how you could have responded differently to achieve a more positive outcome. This exercise helps you gain insights into what triggers you emotionally and develop strategies for managing them more effectively.

Integrating these Stoic strategies into daily interactions can enhance emotional intelligence and improve relationships. Practicing empathy, reflecting on your emotional responses, and developing self-awareness and self-regulation are potent tools for navigating social interactions with wisdom and grace. These practices help you build deeper connections, resolve conflicts more effectively, and maintain a sense of inner peace amid the complexities of human relationships.

HANDLING LIFE TRANSITIONS: STOIC GUIDANCE FOR CHANGE

Life transitions can be some of our most stressful and disorienting experiences. Whether it is a career change, moving to a new city, or navigating a shift in a personal relationship, these significant changes disrupt our routines and challenge our sense of stability. The psychological impact of such transitions is substantial. They can evoke uncertainty, fear, and a loss of control. For instance, switching careers often brings anxiety about new responsibilities and the fear of failure. Moving to a new city can lead to loneliness and the daunting task of building a new social network. Relationship changes, such as a breakup or a new partnership, come with emotional upheaval and adjustment.

Stoic philosophy offers practical strategies for navigating these transitions with grace and resilience. As previously mentioned, one fundamental concept in Stoicism is *amor fati*, or the love of fate. This principle encourages us to embrace everything that happens, seeing it as necessary for our growth. Instead of resisting change, Stoicism teaches us to welcome it as an opportunity. Reflect on past experiences where change led to personal development. This reflection can help you see current transitions as part of a more extensive, joyous journey. For example, recall when a career shift opened new doors and brought unforeseen benefits. By embracing *amor fati*, you learn to love and accept life's unpredictability.

Maintaining a sense of purpose is crucial during life transitions. A clear understanding of purpose provides stability and direction, even when everything else seems uncertain. To identify and reaffirm your purpose, start by reflecting on what truly matters to you— your core values. Consider what drives you and brings you fulfillment. Quotes from Stoic philosophers can offer inspiration. Marcus Aurelius wrote, "The impediment to action advances action. What stands in the way becomes the way." This quote emphasizes the importance of purpose in overcoming obstacles. By focusing on your purpose, you can navigate transitions with a sense of direction and confidence.

Practical exercises can help you apply Stoic principles during life changes. One effective exercise is writing a letter to your future self about your current transition. Describe your hopes, fears, and plans to navigate the change. This exercise helps you articulate your thoughts and create a roadmap for the future. Reflect on how you want to grow and what you hope to achieve.

Another practical example is the story of a professional who navigated a career change using Stoic principles. Faced with the uncertainty of a new job, they embraced *amor fati*, seeing the change as an opportunity for growth. They maintained a clear sense of purpose by focusing on their long-term career goals and values. They successfully adapted to their new role through reflection and purposeful action and found fulfillment.

Exercise: Writing a Letter to Your Future Self About Current Transitions

To deepen your engagement with this practice, set aside time to write a letter to your future self. Describe the transition you are experiencing and how you plan to navigate it. Include your goals, fears, and strategies for maintaining a sense of purpose. Reflect on how you hope to grow through this change. This exercise provides clarity and a motivational tool, reminding you of your resilience and capacity for growth.

Applying these Stoic strategies allows you to navigate life transitions more easily and resiliently. Embracing *amor fati*, maintaining a sense of purpose, and engaging in reflective exercises can transform your approach to change. These practices help you see transitions not as disruptions but as opportunities for personal growth and self-improvement. Through purposeful action and a positive mindset, you can face life's inevitable changes with confidence and composure, turning challenges into stepping stones for a brighter future.

WORKPLACE STRESS: STOIC SOLUTIONS FOR PROFESSIONAL RESILIENCE

Workplace stress is a common issue that many of us face. High workloads and tight deadlines are two significant contributors to this stress. The pressure to meet deadlines often can lead to long hours, sacrificing personal time and well-being. The constant demand to deliver results can be overwhelming, causing anxiety and burnout. Interpersonal conflicts with colleagues also play a significant role in workplace stress. Misunderstandings, differing work styles, and competition can create a tense environment. These conflicts can drain your energy, making it difficult to focus on your tasks. Additionally, the fear of making mistakes or not meeting expectations can add to the stress. This combination of high demands and interpersonal friction creates a challenging work environment that many need help to navigate.

Stoic philosophy offers valuable techniques for managing workplace stress. One of the fundamental Stoic principles is focusing on what is within your control. This means concentrating on your actions, efforts, and attitudes professionally rather than external factors like colleagues' behaviors or company policies. By directing your energy toward what you can influence, you reduce feelings of helplessness and gain a sense of empowerment. Another effective Stoic practice is gratitude. Reflect on the positives in your job, such as learning opportunities, supportive colleagues, or meaningful projects. This shift in focus can help balance the negatives and foster a more positive outlook. It has been proven that gratitude improves mental well-being and resilience, making it a powerful tool for managing stress.

Maintaining composure under pressure is crucial in a high-stress work environment. Stoic principles can help you stay calm and focused during challenging situations. One technique is deep breathing. When you feel overwhelmed, take a moment to breathe deeply. Inhale air through your nose and exhale air through your mouth. This simple breathing practice can clear your mind and calm your nervous system. Visualization is another helpful method. Imagine yourself handling the stressful situation with confidence and ease. This mental rehearsal can prepare you to face the event with more composure. Stoic leaders like Marcus Aurelius exemplified calmness under pressure. As a Roman emperor, he faced numerous challenges but remained steadfast and composed, relying on Stoic principles to guide his actions. His ability to maintain his poise in the face of adversity is a testament to the power of Stoicism in managing stress.

Real-life examples and exercises can illustrate Stoic practices in the workplace. Consider the case of a manager who faced a major crisis at work. A critical project was behind schedule, and the team was under immense pressure. Instead of panicking, the manager applied Stoic principles. He focused on what was within his control, such as organizing the team and prioritizing tasks. He practiced gratitude by acknowledging the team's hard work and dedication. He successfully navigated the crisis by maintaining his composure and guiding the team with a clear and calm mind. This example demonstrates how Stoic techniques can help manage high-stress situations effectively.

Exercise: Reflecting on a Stressful Workday and Identifying Controllable Factors

To apply these principles to your own work life, try this exercise. At the end of a stressful workday, take a few minutes to reflect on the day. Identify the factors that caused stress and categorize them into two lists: those within your control and those outside your control. Focus on the actions you can take to address the controllable factors. For example, if a tight deadline causes stress, consider how to manage your time more effectively or seek colleague support. Reflect on how you handled the stress and think about ways to improve your response in the future. This exercise helps you gain clarity and develop strategies for managing workplace stress more effectively.

Incorporating these Stoic strategies into your daily work routine can build resilience and maintain your well-being in a high-stress environment. Maintaining composure under pressure, practicing gratitude, and focusing on what you can control are potent tools that can transform your professional experience. Whether you are dealing with tight deadlines, interpersonal conflicts, or high demands, Stoic principles offer practical solutions to easier and with more confidence.

MANAGING FINANCIAL STRESS: STOIC APPROACHES TO MONEY

Financial stress is a common struggle. It can significantly impact your mental and emotional well-being. Several factors contribute to financial anxiety, including job instability and economic uncertainty. The fear of losing your job or facing an economic downturn can create a constant undercurrent of stress. This anxiety is compounded by debt and financial obligations. These financial burdens, whether a house mortgage, credit card bills, or student loans, can feel overwhelming. The pressure to meet financial commitments while managing day-to-day expenses can lead to sleepless nights and chronic stress.

You can find practical ways to alleviate this stress by applying Stoic principles to financial challenges. One core tenet of Stoicism is the dichotomy of control, which teaches you to focus on what you can control and accept what you cannot. In financial situations, this means concentrating on your spending habits, saving strategies, and financial planning while accepting that market fluctuations and economic conditions are beyond your control. Reflecting on what is necessary for a fulfilling life is another Stoic practice that can help manage financial stress. Marcus Aurelius often wrote about the importance of distinguishing between needs and wants. By focusing on what you genuinely need, you can reduce unnecessary spending and find contentment in simplicity.

Financial planning and mindfulness are essential components of managing financial stress. Creating a realistic budget is a practical step providing clarity and control over your finances. Start by tracking your income and spending to understand where your money is going. Identify areas where you can cut back and allocate funds toward savings and debt repayment. This proactive approach helps reduce financial anxiety by providing a clear plan for managing your money. Mindful spending and saving are also crucial. Before purchasing, ask yourself if it aligns with your values and long-term goals. This reflection helps you make more intentional financial decisions, reducing impulse buys and unnecessary expenses.

To illustrate these principles, consider the story of an individual who overcame financial stress through Stoic budgeting. They decided to apply Stoic principles to their finances because of significant debt and economic uncertainty. They began by practicing the dichotomy of control, focusing on their spending habits and saving strategies. They created a detailed budget, tracking every expense and identifying areas for reduction. By reflecting on what was necessary for their happiness, they cut out non-essential spending and found contentment in a simpler lifestyle. Over time, their financial situation improved, and their stress levels decreased. This example demonstrates how Stoic principles can provide practical solutions for managing financial stress.

Exercise: Reflecting on Financial Goals and Aligning Them with Stoic Values

To apply these principles to your finances, try this exercise. Begin by making time to reflect on your financial goals. Write down your short-term and long-term objectives, such as paying off debt, building an emergency fund, or saving for retirement. Next, reflect on how these goals align with your values. Consider what is truly necessary for your happiness and fulfillment. Are your financial goals driven by external pressures or by genuine needs? This reflection helps you prioritize your spending and saving in a way that aligns with your values and reduces financial stress.

Integrating Stoic strategies into your financial management can build resilience and reduce anxiety. Practicing the dichotomy of control, reflecting on what is necessary, and creating a realistic budget are powerful tools for managing financial stress. Mindful spending and saving further enhance your financial well-being, helping you make intentional decisions that align with your values. Through these practices, you can navigate financial challenges with greater ease and confidence, finding contentment in simplicity and control in planning.

NAVIGATING SOCIAL MEDIA: STOIC STRATEGIES FOR DIGITAL WELL-BEING

In our digital age, social media has become an essential part of our lives, but its impact on our mental health is a growing concern. Too much social media use can lead to higher levels of anxiety, stress, and a pervasive sense of inadequacy. Studies show that prolonged exposure to the curated lives of others often results in unfavorable self-comparisons. According to a study published by the National Center for Biotechnology Information, social media use can aggravate mental health problems, with factors like time spent and type of activity playing significant roles. The study reviewed multiple papers and found a connection between prolonged social media use and adverse mental health outcomes like depression and anxiety. Modern psychologists emphasize that humans require meaningful social connections for mental well-being, and superficial interactions on social media often fall short.

Stoic strategies offer practical guidance to help you healthily navigate the digital landscape. One of the core Stoic principles is the dichotomy of control, which teaches us to focus on what we can control and accept what we cannot. Apply this principle to your online interactions. You cannot control what others post or how they react, but you can control your response and time on these platforms. Setting boundaries is crucial. Set aside specific times for social media use and stick to them. For example, you may check your accounts only during lunch breaks and avoid them entirely in the evenings. This practice helps create a healthier balance and reduces the compulsive urge to check your phone constantly.

Mindful social media use is another effective strategy. Practicing mindfulness means being present and intentional in your actions. Before you open a social media app, ask yourself why you are doing it. Are you looking for entertainment, information, or validation?

Reflecting on the purpose and value of your interactions can help you make more conscious choices. When you do engage, stay present. Avoid mindlessly scrolling and, instead, focus on meaningful interactions. Comment thoughtfully, engage in discussions, and share content that aligns with your values.

To further enhance your digital well-being, consider regular digital detoxes. Taking breaks from social media can help reset your mind and reduce dependency. Start with short detox challenges, such as a 24-hour break, and gradually extend the duration. During these detoxes, pay attention to your feelings and experiences. Note any changes in your stress levels, mood, and overall well-being. Journaling about these observations can provide valuable insights. Write about how you felt before, during, and after the detox. Reflect on any positive changes and consider incorporating regular detoxes into your routine.

Exercise: Digital Detox Challenge and Journaling

To implement a digital detox, choose a day when you can step away from social media. Inform your friends and family in advance if necessary. During the detox, engage in off-line activities like hiking, spending time with loved ones, or reading. Write in a journal about your experience. Write about any challenges you faced and how you felt without the constant presence of social media. Reflect on the benefits you noticed and consider how to incorporate more mindful and balanced social media use moving forward.

By applying Stoic strategies to your digital life, you can mitigate the negative impacts of social media and enhance your mental well-being. Practicing the dichotomy of control, setting boundaries, and engaging mindfully are actionable steps that help create a healthier relationship with technology. Regular digital detoxes and reflective journaling further support this process, allowing you to navigate the digital world more easily and resiliently.

5

INSIGHTS FROM STOIC PHILOSOPHERS

I magine standing on a balcony overlooking the vast city of Rome, the weight of an empire resting on your shoulders. This was the daily reality for Marcus Aurelius, who ruled the Roman Empire and sought wisdom through Stoicism. His life's work, captured in *Meditations*, offers a window into his inner life and the principles that guided him. These writings are not mere philosophical musings; they are practical reflections born out of the struggles and responsibilities of leadership. Beginning with Aurelius, we will review several Stoic philosophers, past and present, who paved a path for us to follow.

MARCUS AURELIUS: MEDITATIONS ON LEADERSHIP AND PERSONAL GROWTH

Marcus Aurelius was born into a prestigious family in 121 AD and became the Roman emperor in 161 AD. Despite the immense power at his disposal, he is remembered not for tyranny but for his wisdom and virtue. His *Meditations*, written as personal notes to himself, reflect his efforts to live a life of virtue, justice, and wisdom. These writings have become a cornerstone of Stoic philosophy, offering timeless insights into personal growth and leadership.

One of the central themes in *Meditations* is the importance of self-reflection. Marcus Aurelius believed that introspection was crucial for personal growth and ethical behavior. He often used his writings to examine his thoughts, actions, and motivations, asking himself whether they aligned with his values and principles. This practice of self-reflection is not just an exercise in navel-gazing; it is a powerful tool for developing self-awareness and integrity. By regularly examining our inner lives, we can identify areas for improvement and cultivate virtues such as wisdom, courage, and justice.

Another critical theme in *Meditations* is the balance between power and humility. Despite ruling one of the most powerful empires in history, Marcus Aurelius constantly reminded himself of the transient nature of power and the importance of humility. He wrote, "Do not waste what remains of your life in speculating about your neighbors, unless with a view to some mutual benefit. To wonder what so-and-so is doing and why, or what he is saying, or thinking, or plotting, is a waste of time." This focus on humility and self-improvement, rather than gossip or envy, is a lesson that resonates in both personal and professional contexts.

Stoic principles profoundly influenced Marcus Aurelius's approach to leadership. He believed in handling crises calmly and rationally, setting an example for others. The Roman Empire faced numerous challenges during Aurelius's reign, including plagues, wars, and political turmoil. Yet, Marcus Aurelius remained steadfast, applying his Stoic training to navigate these crises with composure. He understood that while he could not control external events, he could control his reactions and decisions. This attitude helped him maintain his sanity and inspired confidence and stability in those he led.

Justice and fairness were also central to Marcus Aurelius's leadership. He believed that a leader should act with the good of the community in mind rather than seeking personal gain. In his *Meditations*, he frequently reflected on the importance of acting justly and treating others with respect and fairness. This commitment to justice is evident in his governance, where he sought to implement equitable and beneficial policies for the empire. His leadership style emphasizes the importance of moral integrity and ethical decision-making, which are relevant today.

To apply Marcus Aurelius's teachings in your own life, consider starting a practice of reflective journaling. Each evening, take a few minutes to write about your day. Reflect on your actions, thoughts, and emotions, and ask yourself whether they align with your values and principles. Use prompts inspired by *Meditations* to guide your reflections. For example, you might ask, "Did I act with wisdom and fairness today? How did I handle challenges? What can I learn from my experiences?" This practice can help you cultivate wisdom, courage, and justice and develop greater self-awareness.

Another practical exercise is to cultivate humility and self-awareness through daily actions. Consciously try to speak less, listen more, and consider others' perspectives before forming judgments. Practice gratitude for your opportunities and responsibilities rather than focusing on what you lack. By incorporating these small, daily practices, you can develop a mindset of humility and continuous self-improvement, much like Marcus Aurelius.

His life and writings offer a wealth of wisdom for anyone seeking to grow as an individual and a leader. By embracing self-reflection, balancing power with humility, and applying Stoic principles to our actions, we can navigate life's challenges with greater wisdom, strength, and peace of mind.

EPICTETUS: THE ENCHIRIDION AND PRACTICAL STOICISM

Epictetus's life story is a testament to the transformative power of Stoic philosophy. Born into slavery in ancient Rome around 50 AD, Epictetus experienced the harshest conditions. Yet, his spirit remained indomitable. After gaining his freedom, he dedicated himself to philosophy, becoming one of the most influential Stoic teachers. His teachings, compiled by his student Arrian in *The Enchiridion*, offer practical advice for living a life of virtue and resilience. Unlike other philosophical texts that may seem abstract or theoretical, *The Enchiridion* is a handbook designed for everyday use, making it accessible and relevant for anyone seeking to improve their life.

One of the cornerstone teachings in *The Enchiridion* is the dichotomy of control. Epictetus emphasized that some things are within our control, such as our opinions, desires, and actions, while others, like our body, property, and reputation, are not. This simple yet profound distinction helps us focus our energy where it can be most effective. For instance, you cannot control whether it rains tomorrow, but you can decide to carry an umbrella. By accepting this fundamental principle, you can significantly reduce your stress and anxiety. You learn to let go of what you cannot change and concentrate on what you can influence, making your life more manageable and peaceful.

Another critical teaching from Epictetus is the importance of accepting events as they happen. Life is full of unexpected twists and turns, and our natural tendency is to resist or wish things were different. Epictetus advised against this. He taught us to accept whatever comes our way, not as passive resignation but as an active engagement with reality. For example, if you lose your job, instead of lamenting your fate, you could see it as an opportunity to find a better-suited position or even start a new career. This mindset fosters resilience and adaptability, letting you face challenges with strength and grace.

Epictetus placed a strong emphasis on personal responsibility. He believed that we cannot control external events, but we can control how we respond to them. Taking ownership of one's actions and reactions is pivotal in Stoic philosophy. By focusing on your responses, you reclaim your power and agency. If someone insults you, it is not the insult that hurts but your interpretation. By choosing to remain unfazed, you maintain your inner peace. You can apply this practice of self-discipline and resilience in various aspects of life, from personal relationships to professional settings, enhancing your emotional well-being and overall quality of life.

To integrate Epictetus's teachings into your daily routine, start with daily reflections on control and acceptance. Each evening, take a few minutes to review your day. Reflect on situations where you felt stressed or anxious. Ask yourself whether these situations were within your control. If they were not, practice letting go. If they were, consider how you could have handled them differently. This exercise helps you internalize the dichotomy of control and trains your mind to focus on what truly matters. Over time, you will find that this practice reduces your stress and enhances your sense of well-being.

Another practical exercise is to cultivate self-discipline. Begin with small, manageable tasks. Set a specific goal, like waking up early or completing a daily workout, and commit to it. The key is consistency. Regularly practicing self-discipline builds mental resilience, making it easier to tackle more considerable challenges. Look at using a journal to track your progress. Write down your goals, note your achievements, and reflect on any setbacks. This process not only keeps you accountable. It also provides valuable insights into your habits and behaviors, enabling you to make more informed choices.

Epictetus's teachings offer a wealth of practical wisdom for navigating the complexities of modern life. By embracing the dichotomy of control, accepting events as they happen, and taking personal responsibility for your actions, you can cultivate a life of virtue, resilience, and inner peace. These principles are philosophical ideals and actionable strategies that can transform your daily experiences and enhance your overall quality of life.

SENECA: LETTERS FROM A STOIC AND HANDLING ADVERSITY

Seneca, a towering figure in Stoic philosophy, wore many hats during his life—statesman, playwright, and philosopher. Born around 4 BC in Córdoba, Spain, Seneca was a highly influential adviser to Emperor Nero. His philosophical writings have endured despite his political entanglements, offering timeless wisdom on navigating life's challenges. His most famous work, *Letters from a Stoic*, is correspondence written to his friend Lucilius. These letters delve into Stoic principles, providing practical advice for living a virtuous and fulfilling life amid adversity.

In *Letters from a Stoic*, Seneca explores several key themes, most notably the importance of mental preparation and cultivating inner peace amid external chaos. He believed life consists of unpredictable events, and mental readiness is the best way to handle them. Seneca often emphasized the value of preparing the mind for potential difficulties. He advised, "He who suffers before it is necessary, suffers more than is necessary." By mentally rehearsing possible challenges, we can mitigate their impact when they do occur. This practice does not mean we should live in constant fear but build resilience by anticipating possible hardships.

Another central theme in Seneca's letters is cultivating inner peace regardless of external circumstances. He argued that true tranquility comes from within and is not dependent on external factors. Seneca wrote, "True happiness is... to enjoy the present, without anxious dependence upon the future." This mindset allows us to maintain calm and composure even when the world is in turmoil. By focusing on our inner state rather than external events, we can achieve a sense of peace that remains unshaken by life's inevitable ups and downs.

Seneca's practical wisdom for handling adversity is evident in his letters and life. One of his key strategies for overcoming personal challenges is to see adversity as an opportunity for growth. He wrote, "Difficulties strengthen the mind, as labor does the body." Seneca viewed hardships not as obstacles but as occasions to build resilience and wisdom. This perspective can be incredibly empowering. For instance, if you face a professional setback, instead of viewing it as a failure, consider what lessons it can teach you and how it can contribute to your personal development.

Seneca also embraced the idea that adversity can be a growth path. He believed that facing and overcoming challenges makes us stronger and more resilient. This is not just theoretical; Seneca's life was marked by political intrigue, exile, and personal loss. Yet, he used these experiences to deepen his understanding of Stoic principles and cultivate a sense of inner strength. His life serves as a testament to the power of Stoic philosophy in navigating adversity.

To apply Seneca's teachings, start with reflective journaling on past adversities. Take time to write about your challenges and how you dealt with them. What did you learn from these experiences? How did they shape your character? By reflecting on past adversities, you can gain vital insights about your strengths and areas for improvement. This practice helps you process past events and prepares you mentally for future challenges.

Another practical exercise inspired by Seneca is mental preparation. Each day, take a few minutes to anticipate potential challenges you might face. Visualize how you would handle these situations with calm and resilience. For example, if you know you have a difficult meeting at work, mentally rehearse how you will respond to various scenarios. This practice helps build mental toughness and reduces anxiety. It lets you approach challenges with a composed and proactive mindset.

Seneca's wisdom offers valuable guidance for handling adversity. By preparing your mind for potential difficulties, cultivating inner peace, and embracing adversity as a path to growth, you can navigate life's challenges with greater resilience and tranquility. These practices, rooted in ancient Stoic philosophy, provide practical tools to achieve a balanced and fulfilling life.

MUSONIUS RUFUS: STOIC TEACHINGS ON ETHICS AND VIRTUE

Musonius Rufus may not be as well-known as Seneca or Marcus Aurelius, but his contributions to Stoicism are profound and enduring. Born around 30 AD, Musonius Rufus was a Roman philosopher who dedicated his life to teaching Stoic principles. He believed philosophy was a theoretical exercise and a practical guide to living virtuously. His teachings focused on ethics and daily conduct, emphasizing that virtue is the only true good. Musonius Rufus saw philosophy as a way to correct errors in thinking and behavior, advocating for a life of simplicity and moral integrity.

One of the critical themes in Musonius Rufus's teachings is the importance of virtue in everyday life. He argued that living a virtuous life was not just for philosophers or scholars but for everyone. According to Musonius, virtue should guide all actions at work, home, or social settings. He believed that ethical living was the foundation of a good life and that by practicing virtue, we could achieve true happiness and fulfillment. This focus on practical ethics set Musonius apart, as he provided concrete advice on incorporating virtue into daily routines.

Musonius Rufus also strongly emphasized ethical living as a Stoic practice. He believed that moral behavior should be the norm, not the exception. For Musonius, this meant living a life of self-control, moderation, and simplicity. He advocated for a modest yet nutritious diet, believing overindulgence weakened the body and the soul. He also emphasized the importance of frugality, arguing that excessive wealth and luxury were detrimental to one's moral character. By living simply and ethically, Musonius taught us to focus on what truly matters—developing our virtues and contributing to the common good.

Education and self-improvement were also central to Musonius Rufus's philosophy. He believed education was essential for cultivating virtue and that learning should be a lifelong pursuit. Musonius argued that education should not be limited to formal schooling but should include practical lessons in ethics and daily conduct. He believed that everyone, regardless of gender or social status, should have access to education. This progressive view extended to his belief in equal education for women, a radical idea for his time. Musonius argued that women possessed the same rational capabilities and virtues as men and should receive the same education.

To embody Musonius Rufus's teachings, start with daily reflections on virtuous actions. Each evening, take a few minutes to reflect on your day. Consider the choices you made and whether they were guided by virtue. Ask yourself questions like, "Did I act with integrity today? Was I kind and just in my interactions?" This practice helps you become more aware of your actions and encourages you to make more ethical choices in the future. By regularly reflecting on your behavior, you can identify areas to improve and develop a more substantial commitment to living virtuously.

Another practical exercise inspired by Musonius Rufus is ethical decision-making. When you are faced with a decision, pause and consider the moral implications. Ask yourself whether the choice aligns with your values and principles. For example, if you are tempted to cut corners at work to save time, consider whether this action upholds your commitment to honesty and integrity. By reflecting on your choice's ethical implications, you can ensure your actions are consistent with your values. This practice helps you make better decisions and strengthens your moral character.

Musonius Rufus's teachings offer valuable insights into ethical living and self-improvement. By focusing on virtue, practicing ethical conduct, and committing to lifelong learning, you can cultivate a life of moral integrity and true happiness. His emphasis on practical ethics and daily conduct makes his teachings accessible and relevant, providing a roadmap for anyone seeking to live a virtuous life.

HIEROCLES: THE CIRCLE OF CONCERN AND COMMUNITY

Hierocles, a Stoic philosopher from the 2nd century AD, made significant contributions to Stoicism, particularly in his focus on community and relationships. While less known than his contemporaries, his ideas have had a lasting impact on the way we understand our social responsibilities. Hierocles believed that our well-being is deeply connected to our relationships with others and that a strong sense of community is crucial for a fulfilling life. His philosophical focus was on how individuals can cultivate empathy and compassion within their social circles, enhancing personal and communal well-being.

One of Hierocles's most influential ideas is the concept of the "circle of concern." This model helps us understand our relationships and community by visualizing them as concentric circles. At the center is the self, followed by circles that include immediate family, extended family, friends, fellow citizens, and humanity. The goal is to expand our circle of concern, moving from self-centeredness to a broader, more inclusive view that encompasses all humanity. By doing so, we develop empathy and a sense of social responsibility, recognizing that our actions have far-reaching impacts. Hierocles's model encourages us to consider how we can support and nurture these relationships, ultimately contributing to a more harmonious and interconnected world.

In Stoicism, community and social responsibility are paramount. Stoics believe that we are all interconnected and that our well-being is tied to the well-being of others. This philosophy promotes mutual support and compassion, encouraging us to act in ways that benefit the community. Practicing empathy within the circle of concern involves actively listening to others, understanding their perspectives, and offering support when needed. It is about looking beyond our immediate needs and seeing the humanity in every person we encounter. This approach fosters stronger community bonds and creates a mutual support network that withstands life's challenges.

To strengthen community bonds, consider integrating strategies that promote empathy and compassion. Start by actively engaging with those around you through small acts of kindness or more significant contributions to communal projects. Volunteering your time and skills can have a profound impact, not just on those you help but also on your sense of purpose and connection. Building strong relationships within your circle of concern also involves open and honest communication. Share your thoughts and feelings with others, and encourage them to do the same. This openness fosters trust and deepens connections, creating a supportive and resilient community.

Reflective journaling is a powerful tool to apply Hierocles's teachings to your relationships. Take time each day to write about your interactions with others. Reflect on how you contributed to these relationships and consider ways to expand your circle of concern. Ask yourself, "Did I act with empathy and compassion today? How can I better support those in my community?" These questions help you stay mindful of your social responsibilities and encourage continuous relationship growth. It also provides a space to process your thoughts and emotions, helping you navigate complex social dynamics more easily.

Practical exercises can further help you embody Hierocles's teachings. One effective exercise is to expand your circle of concern consciously. Start by focusing on your immediate family and close friends. Aim to understand their needs and offer support. Gradually extend this focus to include neighbors, colleagues, and even strangers. Look for opportunities to connect with others and contribute to their well-being. This might involve simple gestures like offering a listening ear or more substantial actions like organizing community events. By actively working to expand your circle of concern, you cultivate a more inclusive and compassionate mindset.

Hierocles's emphasis on community and relationships offers valuable insights for enhancing our social connections. We can build stronger, more supportive communities by understanding and expanding the circle of concern, practicing empathy and compassion, and engaging in reflective journaling and practical exercises. These practices enrich our lives and contribute to the well-being of people around us, creating a ripple effect of positive change.

MODERN STOIC THINKERS: CONTEMPORARY INTERPRETATIONS

In recent years, a resurgence in Stoic philosophy has been led by modern thinkers who have adapted ancient teachings for today's world. Among these influential figures are Massimo Pigliucci and Ryan Holiday. Massimo Pigliucci, a professor of philosophy, has dedicated much of his career to making Stoic principles accessible to a broader audience. His book *How to Be a Stoic* blends classical wisdom with modern scientific insights, providing practical advice for living a virtuous life. Ryan Holiday, a best-selling author and marketer, has popularized Stoicism through books like *The Daily Stoic* and *The Obstacle Is the Way*. His work emphasizes the relevance of Stoic principles in overcoming modern challenges and achieving personal growth.

The importance of their work lies in their ability to help bridge that gap between ancient philosophy and contemporary life. By interpreting Stoic teachings through the lens of modern psychology and self-help, they have made these principles more relatable and actionable. Pigliucci, for instance, integrates cognitive-behavioral techniques with Stoic practices, demonstrating how both can complement each other in managing emotions and enhancing mental well-being. On the other hand, Holiday uses historical anecdotes and practical exercises to illustrate how Stoicism can be applied to achieve success and resilience in various aspects of life, from career to personal relationships.

Contemporary interpretations of Stoic principles have shown how these ancient teachings can be adapted to address the complexities of modern life. For example, the Stoic idea of focusing on what we can control has been integrated into stress management techniques. In today's fast-paced world, external pressures make it easy to feel overwhelmed. Modern Stoics advise practicing mindfulness and setting boundaries to maintain focus on what truly matters. They also highlight the importance of self-discipline and intentional living, encouraging people to set clear goals and align their actions with their values. These adaptations make Stoic principles relevant and practical for navigating contemporary challenges.

The impact of modern Stoic literature has been significant, influencing both the self-help genre and personal development practices. Books like *How to Be a Stoic* and *The Daily Stoic* have become essential for those seeking to improve their lives through philosophy. *How to Be a Stoic* offers a step-by-step guide to incorporating Stoic practices into daily routines, making it accessible to seasoned practitioners and beginners. *The Daily Stoic*, structured as a daily devotional, provides bite-sized wisdom and practical exercises for each day of the year, fostering a consistent practice of Stoicism. These works have broadened the appeal of Stoicism, making it a valuable tool for anyone looking to enhance their emotional resilience and mental clarity.

To apply the teachings of modern Stoics, consider incorporating daily readings from Stoic texts into your routine. Start your day with a passage from *The Daily Stoic*, reflecting on its relevance to your life and how you can apply its lessons. This practice establishes a positive tone for the day and reinforces a Stoic mindset. Another practical exercise is to integrate Stoic principles into your daily life. For instance, practice the dichotomy of control by listing things you can and cannot control each morning. Focus your efforts on what you can influence, and let go of what you cannot. This simple exercise can significantly reduce stress and improve your overall well-being.

Massimo Pigliucci and Ryan Holiday have shown that Stoic philosophy is not just an ancient relic but a living, breathing practice that can enhance our modern lives. Adapting Stoic teachings to contemporary contexts has provided valuable tools for achieving personal growth, resilience, and inner peace. Their work underscores the timeless relevance of Stoicism, demonstrating that its principles can guide us through the complexities of modern life with wisdom and grace.

As we progress, these insights from modern Stoic thinkers will serve as a foundation for exploring more advanced techniques and practices. Integrating their teachings into our daily lives allows us to navigate life's challenges with greater wisdom, strength, and peace of mind.

6

CULTIVATING VIRTUES AND OVERCOMING ADVERSITY

A while ago, I found myself standing at the edge of a quiet lake, pondering the complexities of life. The water was perfectly still, reflecting the sky above with pristine clarity. It struck me that wisdom, like the lake's calm surface, offers a clear and undistorted worldview. This moment of reflection led me to delve deeper into the Stoic virtue of wisdom, understanding its profound impact on making rational decisions and leading a virtuous life.

CULTIVATING WISDOM: PRACTICAL STEPS FOR EVERYDAY LIFE

Wisdom in Stoic philosophy is the cornerstone of rational decision-making and living a virtuous life. Defined as the ability to discern the true nature of things, wisdom guides us in understanding what is good, bad, and indifferent. Marcus Aurelius eloquently captures this when he says, "The happiness of your life depends upon the quality of your thoughts: therefore, guard accordingly, and take care that you entertain no notions unsuitable to virtue and reasonable nature." This quote underscores the importance of wisdom in shaping our thoughts and actions, highlighting its role in achieving a fulfilling and balanced life.

Developing wisdom requires consistent effort and deliberate practice. One effective strategy is continuous learning and self-education. Start by reading and reflecting on philosophical texts. Works by Marcus Aurelius, Seneca, and Epictetus offer timeless insights into human nature and ethical living. As you read, take notes and reflect on how the principles can be applied to your life. This reflective practice deepens your understanding and helps internalize the teachings. Additionally, seek out diverse sources of knowledge. Attend lectures, participate in discussions, and explore different perspectives. This broadens your intellectual horizons and enhances your ability to think critically.

Reflection and critical thinking are essential components of wisdom. They enable us to analyze situations objectively and make informed decisions. Practicing critical thinking involves questioning assumptions and evaluating evidence before forming conclusions. For instance, when faced with a complex problem at work, take a step back and consider all possible solutions. Weigh the good and the bad and consider each option's long-term implications. This analytical approach helps you arrive at a rational and well-thought-out decision. Reflective journaling is another powerful tool. At the end of each day, take a few minutes to write about your experiences, challenges, and the decisions you made. Ask yourself questions like, "What did I learn today?" and "How could I have handled that situation better?" This practice enhances self-awareness and promotes continuous improvement.

Real-life examples illustrate how wisdom can guide us through challenging situations. Consider the case of a business leader navigating a crisis. During a significant downturn, they faced pressure to make quick decisions that could impact the company's future. Instead of reacting impulsively, they took the time to gather information, consult with experts, and reflect on the best course of action. By applying wisdom, they made decisions that stabilized the company and positioned it for long-term success. This example demonstrates how wisdom enables us to navigate crises with clarity and composure.

On a personal level, wisdom can guide everyday decisions. Imagine you are faced with a difficult choice, such as whether to move to a new city for a job opportunity. Instead of focusing solely on the immediate benefits, consider the long-term impact on your happiness and well-being. Reflect on your values and goals and how the decision aligns with them. This thoughtful approach ensures your choices are grounded in wisdom and aligned with your aspirations.

Exercise: Reflective Journaling Prompts

To cultivate wisdom through reflection, try incorporating these journaling prompts into your daily routine:

- What significant decision did I make today, and what factors influenced it?
- How did I apply wisdom in handling a challenging situation?
- What can I learn from today's experiences that will guide me in the future?

By consistently practicing this, you can develop and enhance your wisdom, leading to more rational decisions and a virtuous life. Wisdom, as the foundation of Stoic philosophy, empowers you to navigate the complexities of life with clarity, integrity, and purpose.

PRACTICING JUSTICE: STOIC ETHICS IN ACTION

Justice within the Stoic framework is more than a legal or societal concept; it is a moral virtue that embodies fairness and integrity. The Stoics believed that justice is about treating others with the respect and fairness they deserve. Seneca emphasized this when he said, "Treat your inferiors as you would be treated by your superiors." This idea highlights justice's reciprocal nature and the importance of moral integrity. Justice, for the Stoics, is about ensuring that our actions are fair and that we contribute positively to the community.

To practice justice in everyday life, treat others fairly and respectfully. This means recognizing the worth and inherent dignity of every individual you encounter. Whether it is a colleague at work, a family member, or a stranger, fairness demands that you consider their perspectives and act with kindness. Advocating for ethical practices in the workplace is another way to embody justice. This could involve standing up against unfair treatment or ensuring that company policies are equitable and inclusive. By advocating for justice, you create a fairer and more respectful environment.

Empathy and compassion are integral to practicing justice. Empathy lets you understand and share others' feelings. It fosters a sense of connection and concern. Compassion, on the other hand, motivates you to act on that empathy, striving to alleviate the suffering of others. Developing empathy can be as simple as active listening, where you genuinely focus on what someone else is saying without interrupting or judging. Compassionate actions include helping a colleague with a challenging task or supporting a friend through a tough time. These small acts of kindness and understanding contribute to a harmonious and just community.

One compelling example of justice in action is a whistleblower's story exposing unethical practices in their organization. Despite the personal and professional risks, this individual was morally obligated to ensure justice was served. Their actions led to significant organizational changes, promoting transparency and fairness. This story illustrates the power of standing up for what is right, even under challenging circumstances. Another example is community service initiatives. Individuals who volunteer their time and resources to support those in need embody the Stoic principle of justice. Whether it is organizing a food drive, mentoring youth, or advocating for social justice causes, these actions reflect a commitment to fairness and moral integrity.

Reflection Exercise: Empathy Building

To cultivate empathy, try an exercise in perspective-taking. Think about a recent interaction where you disagreed with someone. Reflect on their point of view and consider what might have influenced their perspective. Write about this experience, focusing on understanding their feelings and motivations. This exercise helps build empathy, which is crucial for practicing justice.

As envisioned by the Stoics, justice is a guiding principle for ethical living. It calls for fairness, respect, empathy, and compassion in all our interactions. Integrating these values into daily life upholds moral integrity and contributes to a more just and equitable society. The stories of individuals who have practiced justice in various contexts can serve as powerful reminders. Our actions can make a significant difference.

DEVELOPING COURAGE: FACING FEARS WITH STOIC STRENGTH

Courage is a pillar in Stoic philosophy, providing the strength to face life's challenges and uncertainties. Courage is confronting fear, pain, and adversity with bravery. It is indispensable for personal growth and resilience. Epictetus emphasized the necessity of bravery by stating, "It's not what happens to you, but how you react to it that matters." This quote underscores the importance of our response to difficulties, advocating for courage in adversity.

To cultivate courage in everyday life, start by setting and pursuing challenging goals. These should push you out of your comfort zone and test your limits. For instance, if public speaking terrifies you, set a goal to present at work or join a local speaking club. You build confidence and resilience by gradually exposing yourself to your fears in controlled settings. This method, known as graduated exposure, involves facing your fears incrementally, starting with less intimidating scenarios and progressively tackling more challenging ones. Over time, this practice reduces fears and enhances your courage to confront difficult situations.

Resilience and mental toughness are closely tied to courage. They enable you to withstand adversity and bounce back from setbacks. Building resilience includes developing a positive mindset and focusing on what you can control. Stress management exercises and mindfulness help maintain mental equilibrium during tough times. For example, practicing deep breathing exercises when you feel overwhelmed can calm your mind and body, allowing you to approach challenges with clear thinking. Maintaining a growth mindset—believing you can improve through effort and learning—fosters resilience. You build mental toughness and perseverance by viewing challenges as avenues for growth instead of insurmountable obstacles.

Consider the story of an athlete who overcame significant adversity to achieve greatness. This individual faced a career-threatening injury that required extensive rehabilitation. Instead of succumbing to despair, they viewed the setback as a challenge. They recovered and returned stronger through relentless training, mental conditioning, and unwavering determination, achieving new personal bests. This story exemplifies how courage and resilience can transform adversity into triumph.

Another powerful example is a professional who decided to take a bold career step by leaving a stable job to start their own business. Despite the uncertainties and risks, they pursued their passion with courage and conviction. They faced numerous challenges, from securing funding to building a client base, but their unwavering determination and resilience kept them moving forward. Today, their business thrives, serving as a testament to the power of courage in achieving one's dreams.

By adding these practices into your daily life, you can develop the courage to face life's challenges head-on. Setting challenging goals, practicing graduated exposure, and building resilience and mental toughness arm you with the tools to confront fear and adversity with bravery. The stories of individuals who have demonstrated courage in various situations serve as inspiring reminders that bravery is not being without fear but the strength to move forward despite it.

EMBRACING MODERATION: BALANCING DESIRES AND NEEDS

In Stoic philosophy, moderation is the virtue that ensures balance and self-control in all aspects of life. It is about finding the middle ground between excess and deficiency and maintaining a harmonious state. Musonius Rufus emphasized the importance of self-control by stating, "He who has self-control is moderate; he who is moderate is in the right state of mind." This quote captures the essence of moderation, highlighting its role in achieving mental and emotional equilibrium.

Practicing moderation requires actionable strategies that can be integrated into daily life. One effective technique is mindful consumption. This involves being aware of your desires and making deliberate choices about what you consume, whether it is food, media, or material possessions. For example, when it comes to eating, pay attention to when your body is hungry and savor each bite. Avoid mindless snacking and opt for nutritious meals that nourish your body. Similarly, practice mindful media consumption by limiting screen time and choosing content that adds value to your life.

Setting boundaries and maintaining them is another crucial aspect of moderation. This means knowing your limits and respecting them. For instance, clear work-life boundaries should be established to prevent burnout. This could involve setting specific work hours and sticking to them, ensuring you have time for rest and leisure. Additionally, practice saying no to commitments that do not align with your priorities. Doing so protects your time and energy, allowing you to focus on what truly matters.

Self-awareness plays a pivotal role in practicing moderation. It involves understanding your desires and recognizing when they become excessive. Techniques for increasing self-awareness include regular self-reflection and mindfulness practices. For example, take a few minutes daily to check in with yourself. Ask questions like, "Am I overindulging in any area of my life?" and "What can I do to restore balance?" Reflective journaling can also enhance self-awareness. Write about your experiences, noting any tendencies toward excess or deficiency. This practice is a way to identify patterns and consciously maintain balance.

Consider the story of a professional who successfully managed work-life balance through moderation. This individual was initially overwhelmed by work commitments, leading to stress and burnout. They regained balance and improved their well-being by setting clear boundaries and prioritizing self-care. They established specific work hours, took regular breaks, and made time for hobbies and family. This approach enhanced their productivity and contributed to a more fulfilling life.

Mindful eating is another practical example of moderation in action. Imagine someone who struggled with overeating and weight gain. Adopting mindful eating practices taught them to listen to their body's hunger cues and make healthier food choices. They savored each bite, ate slowly, and avoided distractions during meals. This shift in behavior led to improved health and a better relationship with food. It also fostered a sense of gratitude and enjoyment in their daily meals.

Reflective Journaling Prompts

To cultivate self-awareness and practice moderation, consider incorporating these journaling prompts into your routine:

- In what areas of my life do I tend to overindulge or neglect?
- How can I create and maintain boundaries to ensure balance?
- What small changes can I make today to practice mindful consumption?

You can embrace moderation and achieve a balanced life by consistently engaging in these practices. Moderation, as envisioned by the Stoics, ensures that our desires and needs are in harmony, leading to greater well-being and inner peace.

RESILIENCE IN THE FACE OF ADVERSITY: REAL-LIFE EXAMPLES

In Stoicism, resilience is the ability to withstand and recover from life's challenges and adversities. Defined as mental toughness and emotional strength, resilience is vital to navigate life's ups and downs. Seneca emphasized the importance of resilience by stating, "Difficulties strengthen the mind, as labor does the body." This quote underscores the idea that facing hardships can fortify our mental and emotional capacities, making us more robust and capable individuals.

Building resilience involves developing mental fortitude and emotional regulation. One effective strategy is practicing stress management techniques and mindfulness. Mindfulness helps you remain present and focused, lessening the impact of stressors. Try engaging in deep breathing exercises when you feel overwhelmed. Inhale deeply through your nose. Hold your breath for a few seconds. Exhale slowly through your mouth. This simple act calms your nervous system and clears your mind. Another practical approach is to create a support network. Surround yourself with people who uplift and encourage you. Share your struggles and seek their guidance. Their support can provide you with the strength to persevere.

The role of mindset and perspective in resilience cannot be overstated. A positive attitude helps you view challenges as opportunities for growth rather than insurmountable obstacles. Cultivating a resilient mindset involves practicing gratitude and focusing on what you can control. Write three things you are thankful for daily in a gratitude journal. This practice shifts your focus from what is going wrong to what is going right to foster a positive outlook. Reflective journaling is another powerful tool. At the end of each day, write about the challenges you faced and how you responded to them. Ask yourself, "What did I learn from this, and how can I apply this lesson in the future?" This reflection helps you gain insights and build resilience over time.

Real-life examples of resilience offer powerful lessons and inspiration. Consider the case of a business leader who faced significant financial challenges. During an economic downturn, their company struggled to stay afloat. Instead of succumbing to despair, they took proactive steps to stabilize the business. They implemented cost-cutting measures, sought new revenue streams, and engaged with their team to find innovative solutions. Their resilience and determination saved the company and positioned it for future growth. This story illustrates how mental fortitude and a positive mindset can turn adversity into opportunity.

On a personal level, resilience can be seen in the story of someone recovering from a major setback, such as a severe illness or injury. Imagine an individual diagnosed with a chronic disease that impacted their ability to work and enjoy life. Instead of giving in to hopelessness, they focused on what they could control. They adopted a healthier lifestyle, sought support from loved ones, and pursued hobbies that brought them joy. Over time, their health improved, and they found new ways to lead a fulfilling life. This personal story demonstrates how resilience and a positive outlook can help overcome even the most daunting challenges.

Reflective Journaling Prompts

To cultivate resilience through reflection, consider incorporating these journaling prompts into your routine:

- What challenges did I face today, and how did I respond?

- What lessons can I learn from today's experiences?
- How can I put these lessons into practice to build resilience in the future?

By consistently doing these practices, you can enhance your resilience and better navigate life's adversities. Resilience, as envisioned by the Stoics, empowers you to face challenges with strength and determination, transforming obstacles into opportunities for growth.

STOIC STRATEGIES FOR DEALING WITH FAILURE

In Stoic philosophy, failure is not seen as a defeat but as a valuable learning opportunity and a growth path. The Stoics believed that experiencing failure helps us understand our limitations, refine our strategies, and ultimately become better individuals. Epictetus captured this sentiment when he said, "It is impossible for a man to learn what he thinks he already knows." This quote highlights that authentic learning often comes from recognizing mistakes and failures. Viewing failure through this lens can transform setbacks into personal and professional development springboards.

Analyzing and reflecting on the experience is crucial to deal with failure effectively. Start by identifying what went wrong and why. Break down the situation into specific components and assess each aspect critically. This detailed analysis helps you pinpoint the exact reasons for the failure, whether it is a lack of preparation, poor decision-making, or external factors beyond your control. Once you have identified the causes, reflect on what you can learn from them. Ask yourself questions like, "What could I have done differently?" and "How can I apply this lesson in the future?" This reflective practice turns failure into a powerful learning tool.

Another effective strategy for managing failure is developing a growth mindset. A growth mindset, made famous by psychologist Carol Dweck, is the idea that abilities and intelligence can be developed through effort and learning. Embrace that failure is not an indicator of your worth but a way to grow and improve. When faced with a setback, remind yourself it is a temporary obstacle and focus on your progress. Celebrate small victories along the way and use them as motivation to keep pushing forward. This mindset shift fosters resilience and perseverance, helping you bounce back stronger from failures.

Resilience and perseverance play a crucial role in overcoming failure. They enable you to face setbacks with determination and continue striving toward your goals. Building resilience involves developing mental toughness and emotional strength. Techniques like mindfulness and stress management exercises can help you be focused and calm during challenging times. For example, practice deep breathing exercises to reduce stress and maintain clarity. Perseverance, on the other hand, requires a steadfast commitment to your goals. Set specific, achievable targets and break them down into smaller, manageable steps. This approach helps you track progress and keep motivated, even when faced with obstacles.

Consider the story of an entrepreneur who experienced a significant failure in their business venture. After years of hard work, a sudden market shift led to the company's collapse. Instead of giving up, they took the time to analyze what went wrong. They identified areas where they could have been more adaptable and resilient. Armed with these insights, they started a new venture, applying the lessons they had learned. This time, their business thrived, becoming a success story built on the foundation of past failures. This example illustrates how resilience and a growth mindset can turn setbacks into opportunities for success.

Another inspiring example is a student who faced academic setbacks. Struggling with poor grades and self-doubt, they could have easily given up. Instead, they sought help from tutors, developed better study habits, and remained committed to their goals. Over time, their efforts paid off, and they achieved academic success. This personal story demonstrates how perseverance and wanting to learn from failure can lead to significant achievements.

Integrating these Stoic strategies into your daily life lets you effectively manage and learn from failure. Analyzing and reflecting on setbacks, developing a growth mindset, and building resilience and perseverance equip you with the tools to turn failures into valuable learning experiences. The stories of people who have successfully overcome failure are potent reminders that setbacks are not the end but the beginning of new opportunities for growth and success.

In this chapter, we have explored various Stoic virtues and strategies for overcoming adversity. From cultivating wisdom and practicing justice to developing courage and resilience, these principles provide practical tools for navigating life's challenges. As we move forward, we will delve into daily practices that further solidify these concepts, helping you cultivate a Stoic mindset in every aspect of your life.

7

PERSONAL GROWTH AND PROFESSIONAL SUCCESS

A few years ago, I attended a workshop on goal setting. The seasoned executive speaker shared his personal story of how he transformed his career by setting clear, actionable goals. He spoke about his journey from a struggling middle manager to a successful CEO. What struck me was his emphasis on aligning goals with personal values and virtues, a concept deeply rooted in Stoic philosophy. This experience was a turning point for me, highlighting the power of purposeful living and the importance of setting goals that resonate with one's core principles.

GOAL SETTING: STOIC METHODS FOR ACHIEVING SUCCESS

In Stoic philosophy, goal setting is not just about achieving external success but about aligning your actions with your inner values and virtues. Seneca often wrote about the importance of purposeful living. He stated, "If one does not know to which port one is sailing, no wind is favorable." This quote underscores the necessity of having clear, defined goals. Without them, you drift aimlessly, at the mercy of external circumstances. Stoic goal setting involves identifying what truly matters to you and directing your efforts toward those objectives.

Setting Stoic goals requires discipline and self-awareness. Begin by defining clear, actionable goals. Break them down into specific, manageable steps. This approach makes the goals less daunting and provides a clear roadmap. For example, to improve your physical fitness, start with small, achievable milestones like committing to a 30-minute workout three times a week. Over time, you can build on these smaller steps to achieve larger fitness goals. The key is to make each step specific and attainable, ensuring steady progress toward your ultimate objective.

Aligning goals with personal values and virtues is crucial in Stoic goal setting. Reflect on what is truly important to you. Does external validation drive your goals, or do they resonate with your inner values? Ensure that your goals reflect virtues such as wisdom, courage, and justice. For example, if you value wisdom, set goals that involve continuous learning and self-improvement. If courage is vital to you, challenge yourself to step out of your comfort zone and take on new opportunities. By aligning your goals with your values, you ensure your actions are fulfilling and meaningful.

Perseverance and resilience play a vital role in achieving goals. The Stoics believed that true success comes from persistent effort and overcoming obstacles. Techniques for staying committed to long-term goals include regular self-reflection and maintaining a positive mindset. Reflect on your progress periodically and celebrate small victories. This practice keeps you motivated and helps you stay focused on your objectives. Additionally, develop a growth mindset by viewing setbacks as learning opportunities rather than failures. This perspective fosters resilience and keeps you moving forward, even when you face challenges.

Overcoming obstacles and setbacks is integral to goal setting. The Stoics taught that obstacles are inevitable. However, how you respond to them defines your character. When faced with a setback, take a step back and analyze the situation. Identify what went wrong and what you can learn from it. Develop a plan to address the issue and move forward. For instance, if you miss a deadline at work, reflect on the factors that contributed to the delay and implement strategies to manage your time more effectively. This proactive approach helps you navigate challenges with grace and determination.

Exercise: Writing a Personal Mission Statement

To solidify your goals, try writing a personal mission statement. This statement should encapsulate your core values, long-term objectives, and the virtues that guide your actions. Reflect on questions like, "What do I want to achieve in life?" and "How do my goals align with my values?" Write a concise statement that constantly reminds you of your purpose and direction.

Consider the story of a professional who successfully achieved their career goals using Stoic methods. Initially working mid-level, this individual aspired to become a senior executive. They began by setting clear, actionable goals aligned with their values of wisdom and courage. They pursued continuous learning, sought mentorship, and took on challenging projects that pushed their limits. Despite facing numerous obstacles, they remained resilient, viewing each setback as an opportunity for growth. Over time, their consistent efforts paid off, and they achieved their goal of becoming a senior executive. Their journey illustrates the power of Stoic goal setting in achieving personal and professional success.

DECISION-MAKING: RATIONAL CHOICES IN PROFESSIONAL LIFE

In professional life, decision-making can often feel like navigating a dense fog. The Stoic approach to decision-making brings clarity and focus, emphasizing rational and thoughtful choices. Rational decision-making in Stoicism involves using reason to evaluate situations objectively, free from the distortions of irrational emotions. Epictetus asserted, "It is not things themselves that disturb us, but our judgments about these things." This highlights the importance of rationality in making decisions. We can navigate complexities with a calm and clear mind by grounding our choices in reason.

Making rational decisions starts with evaluating options and outcomes. Begin by gathering all relevant information, considering various perspectives, and weighing the potential consequences of each option. This comprehensive analysis helps identify the best course of action. One effective technique is the decision-making matrix, where you list your options along one axis and criteria for evaluation along the other. Rate each option based on these criteria; the option with the highest score is often the most rational choice. This structured approach minimizes the influence of emotions and ensures a balanced evaluation.

Minimizing emotional influence is crucial in Stoic decision-making. Emotions cloud judgment and can lead to impulsive choices. To manage this, practice mindfulness and emotional regulation techniques. For instance, if you feel overwhelmed by a decision, take a moment to breathe deeply and calm your mind. This pause allows you to approach the situation with a clear head. Another method is cognitive reframing, where you challenge and reframe irrational thoughts. Ask yourself, "Is this emotion driving my decision, or is it based on reason?" By questioning your emotional responses, you can ensure that your choices are grounded in rationality.

Aligning decisions with Stoic values such as wisdom and justice is essential. Wisdom involves making choices that reflect a deep understanding of the situation, while justice ensures that your decisions are fair and ethical. To practice value-based decision-making, reflect on your core values and how they apply to the decision. For example, if you value honesty, ensure your choices are transparent and truthful. In professional settings, ethical decision-making is paramount. Consider a business leader faced with a dilemma involving financial gain versus ethical practices. They choose the ethical route by prioritizing justice and integrity, even if that means sacrificing short-term profits. This decision upholds moral standards and builds long-term trust and credibility.

Exercise: Decision-Making Matrix for Evaluating Options

To aid in rational decision-making, try using a decision-making matrix. List your options in the top row and evaluation criteria in the side column. Rate each option based on these criteria and sum the scores to identify the most rational choice.

The story of a business leader exemplifies the application of Stoic principles in decision-making. Faced with a challenging situation where they had to choose between cutting executive bonuses or laying off employees, they turned to Stoic values for guidance. Reflecting on justice and fairness, they cut executive bonuses, ensuring that financial constraints were shared equitably. This decision, though difficult, was rooted in ethical considerations and demonstrated a commitment to fairness. By aligning their choices with Stoic values, they navigated the dilemma with integrity and maintained the trust of their team.

In professional life, rational and thoughtful decision-making is a crucial skill. By evaluating options and outcomes, minimizing emotional influence, and aligning decisions with Stoic values, you can navigate complexities with clarity and confidence. The practical steps and real-life examples here offer actionable strategies to enhance decision-making. Embrace these principles and let Stoic wisdom guide your choices, ensuring they are rational, ethical, and aligned with your inner values.

TIME MANAGEMENT: STOIC STRATEGIES FOR PRODUCTIVITY

Time management is a core principle in Stoic philosophy, reflecting the value placed on purposeful living. Seneca emphasized the fleeting nature of time. He famously wrote, "It is not that we have a short time to live, but that we waste a lot of it." This underscores the importance of using our time wisely and effectively. Efficient time management aligns with Stoic teachings, ensuring every moment is spent pursuing meaningful and virtuous goals. You can reach your goals and live a life of purpose by managing your time well.

Begin by prioritizing tasks to manage your time effectively. Identify what matters and zero in on those activities. One practical technique is the Eisenhower Matrix, which categorizes tasks into four quadrants: urgent and important, important but not urgent, urgent but not necessary, and neither urgent nor essential. This helps you prioritize tasks that align with your long-term goals while minimizing distractions from less critical activities. Another method is to break down larger tasks into smaller, manageable steps. This approach reduces overwhelm and ensures steady progress. For instance, divide it into daily or weekly tasks if you are working on a significant project to make tracking progress and staying motivated easier.

Minimizing distractions is another crucial aspect of effective time management. In our digital age, distractions are everywhere, from social media notifications to constant emails. To maintain focus, create a dedicated workspace free from distractions. Use website blockers to limit access to distracting sites during work hours. Additionally, practice time-blocking, where you allocate specific time slots for different tasks. This not only helps you stay focused but also ensures that you dedicate adequate time to each task. For example, set aside specific hours in the morning for deep work and reserve afternoons for meetings and administrative tasks.

A vital aspect of time management is self-discipline. It enables you to stick to your schedule and resist procrastinating. Building and maintaining self-discipline involves setting clear boundaries and consistently adhering to them. One effective technique is the Pomodoro Technique. It is when you work for a set period—typically 25 minutes—followed by a short break. This method enhances focus and productivity. It creates a sense of urgency and provides regular intervals for rest. Overcoming procrastination requires a shift in mindset. Begin by identifying what lies behind your procrastination. Is it a lack of motivation, feeling overwhelmed, or fear of failure? Address these underlying issues and implement strategies to counteract them. For instance, if you procrastinate for fear of failure, remind yourself that every task is an opportunity to learn and grow.

Creating a daily schedule aligned with Stoic principles can significantly enhance your productivity. Begin by writing down your goals and priorities for the day. Allocate time for each task, ensuring that you include breaks and time for self-reflection. Reflect on your progress at the end of each day and adjust your schedule as needed. This practice keeps you on track and fosters a sense of accomplishment and continuous improvement. Consider the story of a professional who struggled with time management and productivity. By implementing Stoic principles, they transformed their approach to work. They began by prioritizing their tasks, focusing on what truly mattered. They minimized distractions by creating a dedicated workspace and practicing time-blocking. Over time, their productivity soared, and they achieved their professional goals more quickly and efficiently.

Exercise: Creating a Daily Schedule Aligned with Stoic Principles

To create a daily schedule aligned with Stoic principles, list your top priorities for the day. Set up specific time slots for each task to ensure breaks and time for self-reflection. Use the Eisenhower Matrix to prioritize tasks and the Pomodoro Technique to maintain focus. Reflect on your progress at the end of the day and adjust your schedule as needed.

Integrating these time management strategies into your daily routine can significantly improve productivity. By prioritizing tasks, minimizing distractions, and maintaining self-discipline, you can make the most of your time and achieve your goals more efficiently. The practical steps and real-life examples here offer actionable strategies to improve your time management skills. Embrace these principles and let Stoic wisdom guide your time, ensuring every moment is spent pursuing meaningful and virtuous goals.

LEADERSHIP: STOIC PRINCIPLES FOR LEADING OTHERS

Stoic philosophy offers a profound framework for effective leadership, emphasizing ethical and compassionate principles. In Stoicism, leadership is not about wielding power but guiding others with wisdom and integrity. Marcus Aurelius captured this beautifully when he said, "Waste no more time arguing about what a good man should be. Be one." This quote underscores the Stoic belief that authentic leadership comes from embodying virtues and leading by example.

To lead effectively with Stoic principles, start by demonstrating the virtues of wisdom, courage, justice, and moderation. Leading by example means consistently acting in ways that reflect these virtues. For instance, in decision-making, prioritize fairness and transparency. When faced with a challenging situation, demonstrate courage by taking decisive action. Show moderation by balancing assertiveness with empathy. By embodying these virtues, you set a standard for your team. A practical strategy is establishing core values that guide your leadership. Communicate these values to your team and ensure your actions consistently reflect them.

Another crucial aspect of Stoic leadership is a supportive and ethical work environment. Create a culture where ethical behavior is the norm and team members feel valued and supported. Actively listen to your team's concerns and encourage open communication. This builds trust and promotes a sense of belonging and mutual respect. Implement policies that promote fairness and equity, such as transparent decision-making processes and equal opportunities for growth and development. Creating an environment prioritizing ethical behavior and support empowers your team to thrive and contribute meaningfully.

Empathy and compassion play crucial roles in Stoic leadership. Understanding and supporting your team members fosters a positive work environment and strengthens relationships. Practice active listening to show that you value their perspectives and experiences. When a team member faces challenges, offer support and encouragement. This could involve providing resources, offering guidance, or simply being present to listen. Compassionate leadership consists of recognizing each team member's humanity and acting to uplift and empower them. For example, when a team member struggles with a personal issue, show empathy by offering flexibility and understanding. This helps them navigate their challenges and builds loyalty and trust.

A compelling story of compassionate leadership can be found in the example of a manager who faced a period of low team morale. They recognized the impact on productivity and well-being and turned to Stoic principles for guidance. They began by actively listening to their team's concerns and demonstrating empathy. They implemented changes that addressed these concerns, such as flexible work hours and opportunities for professional development. They significantly improved team morale and productivity by fostering a supportive environment and leading with compassion. This story illustrates how Stoic leadership principles can transform a team and create a positive, thriving work environment.

Exercise: Reflecting on Leadership Practices and Aligning Them with Stoic Values

To enhance your leadership practices, reflect on your actions and decisions. Ask yourself questions like, "How do my actions reflect Stoic virtues?" and "What can I do to better support my team?" Write down your reflections and identify areas for improvement. This self-awareness helps you align your leadership with Stoic principles and fosters continuous growth.

Stoic leadership is about guiding others with wisdom, integrity, empathy, and compassion. You can create a positive and effective leadership style by leading by example, fostering a supportive and ethical work environment, and practicing kindness and compassion. These practical steps and real-life examples offer actionable strategies to enhance leadership skills. Embrace these principles and let Stoic wisdom guide your approach to leading others.

PUBLIC SPEAKING: OVERCOMING FEAR WITH STOIC TECHNIQUES

Public speaking is a common fear that can paralyze even the most confident individuals. Stoic philosophy offers practical solutions to manage and reduce this fear. Epictetus once said, "Men are disturbed not by things, but by the views which they take of them." This insight emphasizes the power of rational thinking in overcoming fear. When you approach public speaking through the lens of Stoicism, you focus on what you can control—your thoughts, preparation, and mindset. This shift in perspective helps you manage the anxiety that may pop up when speaking in front of an audience.

One of the first steps in overcoming public speaking anxiety is thorough preparation and practice. Begin by familiarizing yourself with your material. The more you know your speech, the more confident you will feel. Break your speech into sections and practice each part until you feel comfortable. This method helps you internalize the content and reduces the likelihood of forgetting key points.

Also, record yourself or practice in front of a mirror, which lets you observe your body language and make necessary adjustments. Another effective technique is to practice in front of a small, supportive audience. This simulates the experience of speaking to a larger group and helps build your confidence.

Managing physical symptoms of anxiety is also crucial. You can calm your nervous system with deep breathing and progressive muscle relaxation. Before stepping on stage, take a few deep breaths. Inhale through your nose. Exhale through your mouth. This simple act can reduce your heart rate and help you feel more centered. Progressive muscle relaxation is tensing and relaxing each muscle group, beginning from your toes and working your way up. This practice reduces physical tension and promotes a sense of calm.

Visualization and mindfulness are powerful tools in Stoic practice that can enhance your public speaking skills. Positive visualization involves imagining yourself delivering a successful speech. Close your eyes and picture yourself on stage, speaking confidently and engaging your audience. Visualize the positive reactions and applause from the crowd. This mental exercise creates a sense of familiarity and reduces anxiety. Mindfulness, on the other hand, helps you stay present. During your speech, focus on your breathing and your words. If your mind starts to wander or anxiety creeps in, gently bring your focus back to the present moment. This practice keeps you grounded and prevents your thoughts from spiraling into negative territory.

Consider the story of a professional who overcame their fear of public speaking using Stoic principles. Initially, they experienced intense anxiety before every presentation. By adopting Stoic techniques, they transformed their approach. They began by thoroughly preparing their material and practicing in front of a mirror. They also visualized their success and practiced mindfulness to stay present during their speeches. Over time, their confidence grew, and they became a compelling and engaging speaker. Their journey illustrates the effectiveness of Stoic techniques in overcoming public speaking anxiety.

Exercise: Practicing Speeches in Front of a Mirror or Small Audience

To build confidence in public speaking, try practicing your speeches in front of a mirror. Observe your body language and adjust as needed. Once comfortable, practice in front of a small, supportive audience. This simulates the experience of speaking to a larger group and helps you build confidence.

By integrating these Stoic techniques into your public speaking practice, you can manage and reduce your anxiety. Preparation, visualization, and mindfulness empower you to approach public speaking with confidence and clarity. The practical steps and real-life examples here offer actionable strategies to enhance public speaking skills. Embrace these principles, and let Stoic wisdom guide you in overcoming your fear of public speaking.

BUILDING CONFIDENCE: STOIC EXERCISES FOR SELF-ASSURANCE

Self-confidence is a cornerstone of Stoic philosophy, promoting self-assurance and inner strength. Seneca once remarked, "A man's worth is no greater than the worth of his ambitions." This quote highlights the importance of self-belief in Stoic practice. When you believe in your capabilities, you are likelier to set ambitious goals and go after them with determination. According to the Stoics, confidence stems from understanding your strengths and accepting your limitations. This balanced view fosters a realistic and resilient self-image, enabling you to face challenges with poise and assurance.

To build self-confidence, start with self-reflection and positive self-talk. Reflect on your past achievements and the strengths that contributed to them. Acknowledge your accomplishments, no matter how small, and remind yourself of these successes regularly. Positive self-talk involves replacing negative thoughts with empowering affirmations. For instance, if you think, "I cannot do this," reframe it to, "I have the skills and determination to succeed." This shift in mindset reinforces your self-belief and gradually builds confidence. Another effective technique is setting small, achievable goals. Accomplishing these goals provides a sense of progress and strengthens your ability to succeed. For example, if you need more confidence about speaking up in meetings, start by contributing a small comment or question. Gradually, as your confidence grows, you can take on more significant speaking roles.

Self-awareness and self-acceptance are crucial for building confidence. Understanding yourself—your strengths, weaknesses, and values—provides a solid foundation for self-assurance. Techniques for increasing self-awareness include mindfulness practices and reflective journaling. Take time each day to reflect on your experiences and emotions. Ask yourself questions like, "What did I do well today?" and "What can I improve?" This practice enhances your self-understanding and helps you identify areas for growth. Self-acceptance, on the other hand, involves embracing yourself as you are. Recognize that everyone has flaws and that these do not diminish your worth—practice self-compassion. Be kind and understanding to yourself as you would to a friend. This balanced view fosters a realistic and resilient self-image, enabling you to face challenges with poise and assurance.

Consider the story of an individual who built confidence through Stoic exercises. This person struggled with self-doubt and often felt inadequate professionally and personally. They began by practicing reflective journaling, focusing on their strengths and achievements. Each evening, they wrote about something they did well that day, no matter how small. Over time, this exercise helped them see their value and capabilities. They also practiced positive self-talk, replacing negative thoughts with affirmations like, "I am capable and worthy." Setting and achieving small goals further reinforced their confidence. For instance, they started by volunteering to lead small projects at work, gradually taking on more significant responsibilities as their confidence grew. Through these Stoic practices, they transformed their self-image and became confident and self-assured.

Exercise: Reflective Journaling on Personal Strengths and Achievements

To enhance self-confidence, try a reflective journaling exercise. Each evening, write about a personal strength or achievement from the day. Focus on what you did well and how it contributed to your success. This practice helps reinforce your self-belief and build a positive self-image.

Building confidence through Stoic exercises involves self-reflection, positive self-talk, self-awareness, and self-acceptance. By understanding and embracing your strengths and achievements, you can develop a resilient self-image and confidently face challenges. The practical steps and real-life examples here offer actionable strategies to enhance self-confidence. Embrace these principles and let Stoic wisdom guide you in building a robust and self-assured self.

8

CREATING A STOIC LIFESTYLE

S everal years ago, I was grappling with the chaos of my daily life. Each day felt like a whirlwind of tasks, obligations, and unexpected events. One morning, as I sat quietly with a cup of coffee, I stumbled upon a quote from Marcus Aurelius: "Waste no more time arguing what a good man should be. Be one." This simple, profound statement resonated deeply with me. It made me realize the importance of structuring my day with intention and discipline, embodying the principles of Stoicism in every action. This realization catalyzed me to develop daily routines that have since transformed my life.

DAILY ROUTINES: STRUCTURING YOUR DAY WITH STOIC PRACTICES

Daily routines form the bedrock of Stoic practice, offering a framework to maintain focus and embody Stoic principles consistently. In *Meditations*, Marcus Aurelius emphasized the significance of daily discipline and writing, "Because most of what we say and do is not essential. Ask yourself at every moment, 'Is this necessary?'" This focus on essential actions is a cornerstone of Stoic living. Historical accounts reveal that Stoic philosophers like Seneca and Epictetus adhered to structured routines. These routines concerned productivity and aligning their actions with values and virtues.

Creating a Stoic daily routine begins with setting intentions each morning. Start your day with a moment of meditation or quiet reflection. This practice helps center your mind and set a positive tone for the day. Sit comfortably in a calm space. Close your eyes and focus on your breath. As you breathe deeply, consider what you aim to achieve regarding tasks and personal growth that day. Reflect on virtues like wisdom, courage, and moderation, and set intentions that align with these values. This morning routine is about planning and grounding yourself in Stoic principles.

Evening reflections are equally important in a Stoic daily routine. At the end of each day, review your actions and thoughts. Find a quiet space to sit and reflect on the day's events. Consider what went well and what could have been better. Reflect on your responses to challenges and how well you embodied Stoic virtues. This practice, inspired by Marcus Aurelius's reflections in *Meditations*, helps you learn from your experiences and continuously improve. It fosters self-awareness and personal growth, reinforcing the lessons of the day.

Consistency and discipline are crucial for maintaining effective routines. A consistent routine builds discipline and resilience, essential traits in Stoic philosophy. Maintaining consistency includes setting specific times for your morning and evening practices. Treat these times as nonnegotiable appointments with yourself. Use reminders or alarms if necessary. Overcoming disruptions requires flexibility and forgiveness. Life is unpredictable, and disruptions will occur. When they do, adapt your routine rather than abandon it. If you miss a morning meditation, find a few quiet moments during the day to reflect. The key is maintaining the practice, even if it could be better.

Practical activities can illustrate the effectiveness of these routines. Consider the example of a morning meditation practice. Every morning, I meditate for ten minutes, focusing on my breath and setting intentions for the day. This simple practice has dramatically improved my focus and sense of calm. It prepares me to face the day's challenges with a clear mind and a positive attitude. Another practical exercise is creating a personalized daily schedule. Begin by listing your daily tasks and responsibilities. Allocate specific times for each task, including your morning and evening reflections. Stick to this schedule as closely as possible and adjust if needed for unforeseen events.

Exercise: Creating a Personalized Daily Schedule

Four steps:

1. **Morning Reflection**: Spend ten minutes each morning in meditation or quiet reflection. Focus on your breath and set intentions for the day. Reflect on virtues like wisdom, courage, and moderation.
2. **Daily Tasks**: List your tasks and responsibilities for the day. Prioritize them based on importance and urgency.
3. **Allocate Time**: Assign specific times for each task. Include breaks and time for reflection. Treat these times as appointments with yourself.
4. **Evening Reflection**: Spend ten minutes each evening reviewing your day. Reflect on what went well and what could have been better. Consider your responses to challenges and how well you embodied Stoic virtues.

By structuring your day with these routines, you will enhance your productivity and align your actions with Stoic principles, fostering a life of wisdom, resilience, and inner peace.

THE STOIC DIET: HEALTHY EATING AND MODERATION

Incorporating Stoic principles into your diet can transform how you approach food and nourishment. Musonius Rufus emphasized that our eating habits are fundamental to self-control and balance. He argued that our throats and stomachs are designed for nourishment, not pleasure, and recommended a diet based on simplicity and moderation. This perspective aligns with the broader Stoic commitment to self-discipline and living in harmony with nature. By adopting a Stoic approach to eating, you can cultivate healthier habits that benefit both your body and mind.

First, consider the importance of balance and self-control in your eating habits. Musonius Rufus advised against gluttony and luxurious eating, advocating for simple, natural, and healthy foods. This means focusing on nourishment rather than indulgence. A balanced diet, in the Stoic sense, includes a variety of foods that provide essential nutrients without excess. It is about eating to live, not living to eat. This approach helps you maintain physical health and mental clarity. It lets you focus on what is truly important in life.

Adopting a Stoic diet involves mindful eating and careful meal planning. Mindful eating involves being fully present during meals, savoring each bite, and recognizing hunger and fullness cues. Begin by getting rid of distractions such as phones or televisions while eating. Take small bites, chew slowly, and appreciate the flavors and textures of your food. This practice not only enhances your eating experience but also helps prevent overeating. Planning balanced meals involves incorporating a variety of whole foods, like fruits, vegetables, whole grains, nuts, and lean proteins. Avoid processed foods and excessive sugars, as they can impair both physical health and mental focus.

The benefits of a Stoic diet are manifold. Physically, eating according to Stoic principles can lead to improved health and energy levels. A rich, whole-food diet nourishes your body with the needed nutrients for optimal function, reducing the risk of chronic diseases. Mentally, a balanced diet enhances clarity and focus. When your body is well-nourished, your mind is sharper, and you can think more clearly. This mental clarity supports better decision-making and emotional regulation, which are critical aspects of Stoic living.

One example of a balanced, Stoic-inspired meal plan might include a breakfast of oatmeal topped with fresh berries and nuts, a lunch of a quinoa and vegetable salad with a light vinaigrette, and a grilled fish dinner with steamed vegetables and a side of brown rice. Snacks could include fresh fruit, yogurt, or a handful of almonds. These meals are simple, nutritious, and satisfying, aligning with Musonius Rufus's dietary recommendations. Practicing moderation in food choices means being mindful of portion sizes and avoiding extremes. It is about finding a balance to support your health without overindulgence.

Tips for Practicing Moderation in Food Choices

1. **Portion Control**: Serve smaller portions to avoid returning for seconds. Use smaller plates to help visually control serving sizes.
2. **Listen to Your Body**: Heed your body's hunger and fullness cues. Eat when you are hungry. Then, stop when you are satisfied, not when you are stuffed.
3. **Choose Whole Foods**: Focus on foods close to their natural state. Your diet should include fresh vegetables, fruits, whole grains, and lean proteins.

4. **Limit Processed Foods**: Reduce processed foods containing high amounts of unhealthy fats, salt, and sugar. These foods can lead to overeating and poor health outcomes.

5. **Enjoy Treats in Moderation**: Allow occasional treats, but keep them infrequent and in small portions. This prevents feelings of deprivation while maintaining overall dietary balance.

By embracing these Stoic dietary principles, you can foster a healthier relationship with food. This approach nourishes your body and aligns with the Stoic values of balance, self-control, and mindful living, contributing to physical well-being and mental clarity.

PHYSICAL EXERCISE: BUILDING STRENGTH AND DISCIPLINE

Physical exercise is significant in Stoic philosophy, aligning seamlessly with the principles of strength and discipline. Epictetus often emphasized the importance of physical training. He famously said, "No man is free who is not master of himself." This quote highlights the Stoic belief that control over one's body is as crucial as control over one's mind. Historical accounts reveal that Stoics like Epictetus and Musonius Rufus viewed physical exercise as a means to maintain health and cultivate self-discipline and resilience. They believed that enduring physical discomfort in training mirrored the mental toughness required to face life's challenges.

Incorporating exercise into your daily life can start with setting clear fitness goals. Start by figuring out what you want to achieve, whether building strength, improving endurance, or enhancing flexibility. After you have your goals, break them down into smaller, manageable steps. For example, to complete a marathon, begin with short distances and gradually increase them. This approach makes the goal more attainable and keeps you motivated. Creating a balanced workout plan is equally essential. Ensure your routine includes cardiovascular exercises, strength training, and flexibility workouts. This balance helps you build overall fitness and prevents burnout.

Discipline and resilience are at the heart of physical training. Regular exercise builds mental toughness, teaching you to push through discomfort and stay committed. Techniques for maintaining exercise consistency include setting a fixed time for workouts and treating it as nonnegotiable. Much like your morning meditation or evening reflection, make exercise a part of your daily routine. Overcoming physical and mental barriers requires a resilient mindset. When faced with obstacles like fatigue or lack of motivation, remember the long-term benefits and your initial goals. Visualization can be a powerful tool; envision yourself achieving your goals and the sense of accomplishment it will bring.

Consider practical activities to illustrate the Stoic approach to physical fitness. A daily workout routine might start with a morning run or a yoga session to invigorate your body and mind. Follow it with strength training exercises, such as push-ups, squats, and planks, which require minimal equipment and can be done anywhere. End with stretching exercises to improve flexibility and prevent injuries. This routine, inspired by Stoic principles, builds physical strength and mental resilience. Reflecting on the benefits of physical training can further reinforce your commitment. Spend a few minutes after each workout to jot down how you feel. Note improvements in your strength, endurance, and overall well-being. This reflection helps you stay motivated and recognize the progress you have made.

Exercise: Reflecting on the Benefits of Physical Training

Steps:

1. **Post-Workout Reflection**: Find a quiet space to sit and reflect after completing your workout.
2. **Journal Entry**: Write about the physical sensations you experienced during the workout. Did you feel stronger, more energized, or more flexible?
3. **Mental and Emotional Benefits**: Reflect on how the exercise impacted your mood and mental state. Did you feel more focused, less stressed, or more resilient?
4. **Progress Tracking**: Note any improvements or milestones achieved. Have you increased your running distance, lifted heavier weights, or held a plank longer?

By consistently reflecting on these aspects, you reinforce the positive outcomes of physical training, making it easier to remain committed to your fitness goals. The Stoic approach to exercise is not about achieving perfection but about continuous improvement and resilience. As Epictetus said, "No great thing is created suddenly." This principle applies to physical fitness as much as it does to any other aspect of life.

COMMUNITY AND RELATIONSHIPS: APPLYING STOIC PRINCIPLES SOCIALLY

Community and relationships lie at the heart of Stoic philosophy. Hierocles, a Stoic philosopher, introduced the concept of the circle of concern, which illustrates the importance of expanding our empathy and compassion. He visualized relationships as concentric circles, starting from the self and extending outward to include family, friends, fellow citizens, and eventually all of humanity. This model encourages us to draw people from the outer circles into our inner circles, fostering a sense of interconnectedness and mutual support. Empathy and compassion are vital in this process because they allow us to deeply understand and care for others.

Applying Stoic principles in social interactions begins with practicing empathy and understanding. One effective technique is active listening. When engaging with others, focus entirely on what they say without interrupting or planning your response. This displays respect and helps you better understand their perspective. Another method is to put yourself in their shoes. Imagine how you would feel in their situation and respond with compassion and kindness. These practices strengthen relationships and align with the Stoic virtues of justice and wisdom.

Resolving conflicts with Stoic calmness involves maintaining composure and focusing on rational solutions. When disagreements arise, take a moment to breathe deeply and calm your mind. Approach the situation with a focus on facts rather than emotions. Use "I" statements to express your feelings and not blame the other person, like, "I feel concerned when meetings start late because it affects my schedule." This approach fosters constructive dialogue and helps resolve conflicts amicably. The goal is to seek understanding and find common ground, reflecting the Stoic commitment to fairness and harmony.

Strong community ties offer numerous benefits, contributing to personal growth and resilience. A supportive community gives a sense of belonging and mutual support, which is essential for navigating life's challenges. Engaging in community service is an excellent way to embody Stoic principles. Volunteering for local charities, organizing community clean-up events, or mentoring young people exemplify actionable Stoic values. These activities benefit others and enrich your life, fostering a sense of purpose and fulfillment.

The benefits of mutual support and shared values in a community are profound. You feel understood and validated when you are part of a community that shares your values. This support network can offer guidance, encouragement, and practical help during difficult times. For instance, being part of a Stoic study group or community can provide a space to discuss Stoic teachings, share experiences, and support each other's growth. These interactions strengthen your commitment to Stoic principles and enhance your personal development.

Consider a practical example of a community project inspired by Stoic values. Imagine organizing a neighborhood garden where residents gather to plant and maintain a communal space. This project promotes cooperation, environmental stewardship, and a sense of shared responsibility. It also provides a venue for fostering relationships and practicing Stoic virtues like patience, perseverance, and gratitude. Such initiatives create a stronger, more connected community.

Exercise: Reflecting on Personal Relationships and Areas for Improvement

Take some time to reflect on your relationships. Think about your interactions with family, friends, colleagues, and neighbors. Are there areas where you could practice more empathy and understanding? Identify specific actions to improve these relationships. Write down your reflections and make a plan to implement these changes. This exercise helps you apply Stoic principles in your social life, enhancing your relationships and building a stronger sense of community.

Integrating these Stoic practices into social interactions improves relationships and contributes to a more compassionate and connected community. Empathy, understanding, and mutual support align with the Stoic commitment to living a virtuous and meaningful life.

LIFELONG LEARNING: CONTINUING YOUR STOIC PATH

Lifelong learning is a cornerstone of Stoic philosophy. Seneca often spoke about the value of ongoing education. He famously said, "As long as you live, keep learning how to live." This quote underscores the importance of continuous self-improvement. In the historical context of Stoicism, education was not just about accumulating knowledge. It was also about cultivating wisdom and virtue. Stoic philosophers believed that learning should be an unending pursuit to understand the world and improve oneself.

Engaging in lifelong learning involves setting clear learning goals. Start by identifying areas you want to explore or skills you wish to develop. These goals should be aligned with your values, specific, and measurable. For instance, to deepen your understanding of Stoic philosophy, set a goal to read one Stoic text each month. Accessing diverse educational resources is crucial. Utilize books, online courses, podcasts, and lectures to expand your knowledge. Libraries, educational platforms like Coursera or Khan Academy, and podcasts on Stoic philosophy can be invaluable tools in this process. The key is to remain steadfastly committed and consistent in your learning efforts.

Curiosity and open-mindedness play significant roles in lifelong learning. Maintaining a curious mind means constantly asking questions and seeking answers. It involves being open to new ideas and perspectives, even those that challenge your beliefs. Techniques for cultivating curiosity include reading widely, engaging in discussions, and exploring topics outside your comfort zone. Methods for expanding knowledge and perspectives involve seeking out diverse viewpoints and experiences. Traveling, meeting new people, and participating in cultural activities can all contribute to a broader understanding of the world. This openness enriches your knowledge and fosters empathy and compassion, aligning with Stoic virtues.

Consider the example of a self-directed learning project to illustrate effective lifelong learning practices. Imagine you have a keen interest in ancient philosophy. Start by creating a reading list that includes works by Plato, Aristotle, and Stoic philosophers like Epictetus and Marcus Aurelius. Set aside dedicated time each week for reading and reflection. Take notes, and consider joining a study group to discuss your insights. This project deepens your understanding of philosophy and enhances your analytical and critical thinking skills. It is a practical demonstration of how continuous learning can be structured and flexible, allowing you to explore your interests deeply.

Exercise: Creating a Personal Learning Plan

1. **Identify Learning Goals**: Write down specific areas you want to learn about or skills you wish to develop. Ensure these goals are clear and achievable.
2. **Access Resources**: List the books, courses, podcasts, and other resources you will use. Be diverse in your choices to get a well-rounded perspective.
3. **Set a Schedule**: Allocate specific times each week for learning activities. Treat this time as a priority, much like your daily routines.
4. **Reflect** and Adjust: Review your progress regularly. Reflect on what you have learned and adjust your plan as needed.

Engaging in lifelong learning through these methods aligns with Stoic principles and fosters a more prosperous, more fulfilling life. You continuously grow and evolve by setting clear goals, accessing diverse resources, and maintaining curiosity. This relentless pursuit of knowledge and wisdom is a testament to the Stoic commitment to self-improvement and virtue.

BUILDING A STOIC SUPPORT NETWORK: FINDING LIKE-MINDED INDIVIDUALS

Connecting with like-minded individuals can profoundly enhance your Stoic practice. Epictetus emphasized the importance of companionship, stating, "Associate with those who will make a better man of you." This underscores the value of mutual support in Stoic practice. A network of Stoic practitioners provides encouragement, shared learning, and accountability. In this interconnected age, finding such a network is easier than ever.

Start by identifying like-minded individuals. Join forums or social media groups online about Stoicism. Platforms like Reddit, Facebook, and specialized forums offer vibrant communities where you can connect with others who share your interest in Stoic philosophy. Local meetups and Stoic events are also excellent opportunities. Websites like Meetup.com often list gatherings where you can meet fellow Stoics. Initiate conversations. Be open to learning from others by asking questions, and sharing your experiences, and

Fostering supportive relationships within this network involves active engagement. Regularly contribute to discussions, offer support and encouragement, and share valuable resources. Building a supportive network works both ways. Offer your insights and be receptive to feedback. Over time, these interactions build trust and camaraderie. Consider starting a Stoic study group. Invite a few like-minded individuals to meet in person or virtually regularly to discuss Stoic texts and reflect on their application in daily life. This creates a structured environment for shared learning and growth.

The benefits of a Stoic support network are immense. Having a group of Stoic practitioners provides a sense of belonging and mutual support. When you face challenges, your network can offer encouragement and practical advice based on Stoic principles. Shared learning within the group enhances everyone's understanding and application of Stoicism. For instance, a member might share a personal story of how they applied the dichotomy of control in a difficult situation, offering insights and inspiration to others.

Support networks also provide accountability. When you commit to practicing Stoic principles, having a group to check in with helps you stay on track. Sharing your goals and progress with the group creates a sense of responsibility. If you need more consistency in your Stoic practices, your network can offer encouragement and practical tips to help you stay committed. This mutual accountability strengthens everyone's resolve to live according to Stoic virtues.

An example of a Stoic study group illustrates these benefits. Imagine a small group that meets weekly to discuss a chapter from Marcus Aurelius's *Meditations*. Each member shares their reflections, challenges, and insights. The group offers diverse perspectives and practical advice, enriching everyone's understanding of the text. Over time, members develop strong bonds, supporting each other in their Stoic practices and personal growth.

Exercise: Reflecting on the Value of Supportive Relationships

Take a moment to reflect on the supportive relationships in your life. Think about how these relationships have influenced your personal growth and resilience. Write down the names of individuals who have supported you and describe specific instances where their support made a difference. Reflect on how you can foster and strengthen these relationships further. This exercise highlights the importance of a supportive network and encourages you to nurture these connections actively.

Building a Stoic support network enhances your practice and enriches your life with meaningful connections. By actively seeking and fostering supportive relationships, you create a strong base for continuous growth and resilience, aligning with the Stoic commitment to living a virtuous and fulfilling life.

This chapter explored how to structure your day with Stoic practices, adopt a healthy and moderate diet, build strength and discipline through physical exercise, enhance social interactions and community involvement, engage in lifelong learning, and find like-minded individuals for mutual support. These practices, rooted in Stoic principles, offer a comprehensive approach to living a balanced, resilient, and fulfilling life. Next, we delve into the practical application of these principles in navigating modern life's complexities, providing actionable strategies for integrating Stoicism into your daily routine.

CONCLUSION

As we reach the end of our journey through the advanced techniques of Stoic philosophy, let's reflect on the key components that can transform your life. We have delved into the depths of Stoic principles and explored how these ancient teachings can be applied to modern-day challenges.

At the core of Stoicism lies its advanced philosophy. We have explored virtue ethics, emphasizing the importance of developing moral character and living by nature. The concept of the dichotomy of control teaches you to focus on what you can control—your thoughts and actions—while accepting what is beyond your control. This powerful mindset shift can significantly reduce stress and anxiety. The Stoic view of fate, encapsulated in the idea of *amor fati*, encourages you to embrace life's challenges with acceptance and resilience.

Building emotional resilience is a cornerstone of Stoic practice. Techniques like cognitive reframing allow you to change your perspective on challenging situations, turning obstacles into opportunities for growth. *Premeditatio malorum,* contemplating potential misfortunes, prepares you mentally for adversity. This foresight enables you to face difficulties with a composed and resilient mindset.

Meditation and reflection are integral to internalizing Stoic teachings. Morning meditation establishes a positive tone for the day, aligning your mind with Stoic principles. Evening reflection helps you review your actions and thoughts, fostering self-awareness and personal growth. Journaling, a daily Stoic practice, allows you to track your progress and cultivate emotional resilience. Visualization techniques, like negative visualization, help you appreciate what you have and prepare for future challenges.

In applying Stoicism to modern life, you have learned strategies for navigating social media, managing workplace stress, handling life transitions, and building emotional intelligence. These practical applications demonstrate the timeless relevance of Stoic principles, helping you navigate today's complexities with wisdom and resilience.

Insights from Stoic philosophers like Marcus Aurelius, Epictetus, Seneca, Musonius Rufus, and Hierocles offer valuable lessons. Marcus Aurelius's *Meditations* teaches the importance of self-reflection and humility in leadership. Epictetus's *The Enchiridion* emphasizes personal responsibility and the dichotomy of control. Seneca's *Letters from a Stoic* provides wisdom on mental preparation and inner peace. Musonius Rufus highlights the importance of virtue in daily life, while Hierocles's circle of concern stresses empathy and community.

Cultivating virtues and overcoming adversity are essential aspects of Stoic practice. Wisdom, justice, courage, and moderation guide your actions, helping you navigate life's challenges with integrity and strength. Resilience in adversity builds mental toughness, enabling you to learn from failures and grow stronger.

Aligning your actions with Stoic principles can lead to personal growth and professional success. Setting goals that reflect your values and virtues leads to purposeful living. Rational decision-making, effective time management, and ethical leadership are critical to Stoic success. Overcoming public speaking anxiety and building confidence through Stoic exercises enhance your professional capabilities.

Creating a Stoic lifestyle involves structuring your day with Stoic practices, adopting a healthy diet, incorporating physical exercise, and building strong community ties. Lifelong learning and finding like-minded individuals for support are crucial for continuous personal growth. These elements create a balanced, resilient, and fulfilling life.

As you insert these practices into your daily routine, you will find that Stoicism offers a practical and robust framework for living with wisdom, strength, and inner peace. Remember, the journey of Stoic practice is ongoing. Continuously reflect on your actions, learn from experiences, and strive to embody Stoic virtues in every aspect of your life.

In closing, I encourage you to act. Start with small, manageable steps. Practice morning meditation, engage in mindful eating, or join a Stoic community. These actions will set you on a path of personal growth and resilience. Embrace life's challenges and opportunities, knowing you have the tools to navigate them with a Stoic mindset.

Reflect on this quote from Marcus Aurelius, which we began with: "You have power over your mind—not outside events. Realize this, and you will find strength." Let this wisdom guide you as you continue your journey. Embrace Stoic principles, cultivate virtues, and strive for a life of wisdom, resilience, and inner peace.

As I wrote this book, I aimed to empower you to navigate life's challenges with courage and wisdom. I hope the insights and practices shared here inspire a lifelong journey of self-reliance and personal growth. Thank you for embarking on this path with me. May you continue to gain wisdom, strength, and peace.

FURTHER READING

The Daily Stoic, Ryan Holiday

The Enchiridion, Epictetus

The Handbook of Virtue Ethics, Stan van Hooft

"How Stoicism Could Help You Build Resilience," Donald J. Robinson, Psychology Today, https://www.psychologytoday.com/us/blog/the-psychology-stoicism/202208/how-stoicism-could-help-you-build-resilience

How to Be a Stoic, Massimo Pigliucci

Letters from a Stoic, Seneca

"Musonius Rufus," William O. Stephens, The Internet Encyclopedia of Philosophy, https://iep.utm.edu/musonius/

The Obstacle Is the Way, Ryan Holiday

"Social Media Use and Its Connection to Mental Health: A Systematic Review," Fazida Karim, et al., *Cureus*, https://www.ncbi.nlm.nih.gov/pmc/articles/PMC7364393/

"The Western origins of mindfulness therapy in ancient Rome," Andrea E. Cavanna, et al., *Neurological Sciences*, https://www.ncbi.nlm.nih.gov/pmc/articles/PMC10175387/